Public Shaming

Other Books of Related Interest

Opposing Viewpoints Series
Civil Liberties
Ethics
Privacy
Understanding and Engaging Humanity

At Issue Series
Are Social Networking Sites Harmful?
Cyberbullying
Does the Internet Increase Anxiety?
Is Society Becoming Less Civilized?

Current Controversies Series
Bullying
Cybercrime
Internet Activism
Media Ethics

> "Congress shall make no law … abridging the freedom of speech, or of the press."

First Amendment to the US Constitution

The basic foundation of our democracy is the First Amendment guarantee of freedom of expression. The Opposing Viewpoints series is dedicated to the concept of this basic freedom and the idea that it is more important to practice it than to enshrine it.

OPPOSING VIEWPOINTS® SERIES

| Public Shaming

Anne Cunningham, Book Editor

GREENHAVEN PUBLISHING

Published in 2017 by Greenhaven Publishing, LLC
353 3rd Avenue, Suite 255, New York, NY 10010

Copyright © 2017 by Greenhaven Publishing, LLC

First Edition

Articles in Greenhaven Publishing anthologies are often edited for length to meet page
requirements. In addition, original titles of these works are changed to clearly present
the main thesis and to explicitly indicate the author's opinion. Every effort is made to
ensure that Greenhaven Publishing accurately reflects the original intent of the authors.
Every effort has been made to trace the owners of the copyrighted material.

Cover image: altanaka/Shutterstock.com

Library of Congress Cataloging-in-Publication Data

Names: Cunningham, Anne.
Title: Public shaming / Anne Cunningham.
Description: New York : Greenhaven Publishing, 2017. |
Series: Opposing viewpoints | Includes index.
Identifiers: LCCN ISBN 9781534500334 (pbk.) | ISBN 9781534500235 (library bound)
Subjects: LCSH: Shame—Juvenile literature. | Public opinion—Juvenile
literature. | Self-actualization (Psychology)—Juvenile literature.
Classification: LCC BF575.S45 C75 2017 | DDC 303.3'8—dc23

Manufactured in the United States of America

Website: http://greenhavenpublishing.com

Contents

Chapter 1: Is Public Shaming Needed in Today's Society?

Chapter 2: Is Public Shaming an Effective Disciplinary Tool?

Chapter 3: Should the Media Engage in Public Shaming?

Chapter 4: Is Public Shaming an Appropriate Means of Punishing Criminal Offenders?

The Importance of Opposing Viewpoints

Perhaps every generation experiences a period in time in which the populace seems especially polarized, starkly divided on the important issues of the day and gravitating toward the far ends of the political spectrum and away from a consensus-facilitating middle ground. The world that today's students are growing up in and that they will soon enter into as active and engaged citizens is deeply fragmented in just this way. Issues relating to terrorism, immigration, women's rights, minority rights, race relations, health care, taxation, wealth and poverty, the environment, policing, military intervention, the proper role of government—in some ways, perennial issues that are freshly and uniquely urgent and vital with each new generation—are currently roiling the world.

If we are to foster a knowledgeable, responsible, active, and engaged citizenry among today's youth, we must provide them with the intellectual, interpretive, and critical-thinking tools and experience necessary to make sense of the world around them and of the all-important debates and arguments that inform it. After all, the outcome of these debates will in large measure determine the future course, prospects, and outcomes of the world and its peoples, particularly its youth. If they are to become successful members of society and productive and informed citizens, students need to learn how to evaluate the strengths and weaknesses of someone else's arguments, how to sift fact from opinion and fallacy, and how to test the relative merits and validity of their own opinions against the known facts and the best possible available information. The landmark series Opposing Viewpoints has been providing students with just such critical-thinking skills and exposure to the debates surrounding society's most urgent contemporary issues for many years, and it continues to serve this essential role with undiminished commitment, care, and rigor.

The key to the series's success in achieving its goal of sharpening students' critical-thinking and analytic skills resides in its title—

Opposing Viewpoints. In every intriguing, compelling, and engaging volume of this series, readers are presented with the widest possible spectrum of distinct viewpoints, expert opinions, and informed argumentation and commentary, supplied by some of today's leading academics, thinkers, analysts, politicians, policy makers, economists, activists, change agents, and advocates. Every opinion and argument anthologized here is presented objectively and accorded respect. There is no editorializing in any introductory text or in the arrangement and order of the pieces. No piece is included as a "straw man," an easy ideological target for cheap point-scoring. As wide and inclusive a range of viewpoints as possible is offered, with no privileging of one particular political ideology or cultural perspective over another. It is left to each individual reader to evaluate the relative merits of each argument— as he or she sees it, and with the use of ever-growing critical-thinking skills—and grapple with his or her own assumptions, beliefs, and perspectives to determine how convincing or successful any given argument is and how the reader's own stance on the issue may be modified or altered in response to it.

This process is facilitated and supported by volume, chapter, and selection introductions that provide readers with the essential context they need to begin engaging with the spotlighted issues, with the debates surrounding them, and with their own perhaps shifting or nascent opinions on them. In addition, in conjunction with the goals of Common Core curriculum standards, guided reading and discussion questions encourage readers to determine the authors' point of view and purpose, interrogate and analyze the various arguments and their rhetoric and structure, evaluate the arguments' strengths and weaknesses, test their claims against available facts and evidence, judge the validity of the reasoning, and bring into clearer, sharper focus the reader's own beliefs and conclusions and how they may differ from or align with those in the collection or those of their classmates.

Research has shown that reading comprehension skills improve dramatically when students are provided with compelling, intriguing, and relevant "discussable" texts. The subject matter of these collections could not be more compelling, intriguing, or urgently relevant to today's students and the world they are poised to inherit. The anthologized articles and the reading and discussion questions that are included with them also provide the basis for stimulating, lively, and passionate classroom debates. Students who are compelled to anticipate objections to their own argument and identify the flaws in those of an opponent read more carefully, think more critically, and steep themselves in relevant context, facts, and information more thoroughly. In short, using discussable text of the kind provided by every single volume in the Opposing Viewpoints series encourages close reading, facilitates reading comprehension, fosters research, strengthens critical thinking, and greatly enlivens and energizes classroom discussion and participation. The entire learning process is deepened, extended, and strengthened.

For all of these reasons, Opposing Viewpoints continues to be exactly the right resource at exactly the right time—when we most need to provide readers with the critical-thinking tools and skills that will not only serve them well in school but also in their careers and their daily lives as decision-making family members, community members, and citizens. This series encourages respectful engagement with and analysis of opposing viewpoints and fosters a resulting increase in the strength and rigor of one's own opinions and stances. As such, it helps make readers "future ready," and that readiness will pay rich dividends for the readers themselves, for the citizenry, for our society, and for the world at large.

Introduction

According to the interdisciplinary field known as affect theory, shame is foremost among the so-called "negative" emotions. These include feelings such as rage, fear, anxiety, and humiliation. While negative emotions are certainly unpleasant for those experiencing them, they are not wholly unproductive. For instance, without fear to warn us of danger, our species might not have survived threats to its existence. Although shame works a little differently, it, too, plays a vital role in our social evolution.

Primarily, shame is a tool through which social conventions are enforced. Because social norms change over time and are not consistent across cultures, it is useful to evaluate whether social norms serve the common good or simply encourage conformity to an existing power structure. To take a familiar example, it is now acceptable to raise a child out of wedlock in many societies. However, this was not always the case. In Nathaniel Hawthorne's novel *The Scarlet Letter*, protagonist Hester Prynne was forced to emblazon the letter "A" on her person as a mark of shame to brand her as an adulterer among the Puritans in her colonial community. Even today in some communities, having an illegitimate child is judged by individuals to be a shameful act even though it arguably does nothing to hurt the common good.

By contrast, offensive words from public figures, malfeasance committed by financial institutions, and environmental degradation wreaked by corporations are clearly detrimental to the public good. Experts such as Jennifer Jacquet argue that public shaming is an effective way to discourage bad behavior. If enough people shame corporations that pollute, for example, this would force these companies to be accountable and potentially influence their practices for the better. Therefore, it is crucial to distinguish the purposeful shaming of institutions from "call-outs"—the vicious and often self-righteous shaming of individuals who exercise woefully poor judgment.

Most of us agree there should be no space for discriminatory and hateful personal expression. Yet, we know this occurs. Ignorant, racist, and sexist people walk (and tweet) among us on a daily basis. When a person is caught blatantly engaging in such anti-social behavior, those who "know better" often gang up and vent their exaggerated moral outrage upon the perpetrator. The rampant public shaming of individuals we see today, particularly online, is perhaps symptomatic of our collective frustration with a society that has failed to live up to its ideals. The Obama presidency was said to usher in the beginning of post-racial America, while feminist, LGBTQ, and allied movements sought the transformation of white male hegemony. Nonetheless, much material compiled online reveals a marked lack of progress. If America has in some ways become a more progressive nation, millions among us are enacting a backlash. Will shaming enlighten those predisposed to intolerance, or will it merely further entrench their views?

Proportionality is another recurring concept within the discussion of public shaming. Simply put, this means that the punishment should fit the crime. It also means that a relatively unknown person saying something offensive should not be shamed to the same degree as a powerful media personality airing similar views. This is of particular concern given the near impossibility of expunging information from the internet once it goes public. A person who is involved in a shaming incident may find that the experience follows him or her around forever, making employment and other basics of life problematic. This violates proportionality and fairness.

Both online and off, shaming is now being used on the most dependent among us—children. While shame is effective at altering behavior in the short term, it is a notoriously bad tool for fostering learning and positive emotional development. Yet, we still see parents shaming their children, and teachers calling out struggling students in the classroom. Although few argue these practices should become more widespread, some kids begrudgingly report that shaming works, especially on social media. However, in rare cases this tactic can have tragic results. In fact, one girl even committed suicide after being shamed online. How much the shaming incident contributed to this is unknown, but this tragedy reveals the sensitivity of the adolescent psyche and surely casts doubt on the value of shame as a disciplinary tool.

Finally, the criminal justice system has recently turned to shaming criminals as an alternative form of punishment. Due to factors such as overcrowded jails, judges are sentencing minor offenders to embarrassing sentences such as holding sandwich boards announcing their offense. Legal scholars are split on the efficacy of this trend, although the consensus is that this is both constitutional and likely to increase.

The articles that follow encourage us to thoughtfully parse when, where, and how the "negative" emotion of shame can be harnessed for good reasons. Public shaming has always been part of our society, and it is unlikely to disappear. In fact, the anonymity of the internet will only embolden us to shame our virtual neighbors with growing impunity. This makes a measured and responsible view of shaming essential, and we hope this volume of Opposing Viewpoints facilitates this discussion.

OPPOSING VIEWPOINTS® SERIES

CHAPTER 1

Is Public Shaming Needed in Today's Society?

Chapter Preface

Public shaming is on the rise. In the following pages, we will examine a few now famous instances in which social media users found their lives and careers ruined after an ill-considered remark went viral. Meanwhile, parents are taking to social media to discipline and embarrass their children, sometimes pushing them over the edge during a vulnerable stage in their development. Finally, judges are meting out unorthodox sentences using public shame rather than prison or fines to punish convicts. Is all this shaming encouraging better behavior, or is it a problematic expression of an angry, fragmented, and depersonalized society? Furthermore, how has the internet contributed to this new paradigm, one we might identify as "shame first and ask questions later"?

In the past, mob justice has been a cause for alarm. Today, anyone with a computer and internet access can easily become part of an angry mob from the comfort of their own home. While mob justice looks different in contemporary society, it can be similarly destructive. When words are taken out of context and broadcast by a more powerful and influential internet presence for the thrill of expanding an audience by humiliating a relatively unknown person, this becomes a kind of cyberbullying. And while we certainly should not condone hateful speech, proportionality of response is key. Unfortunately, once an episode catches fire on the internet, any chance at a proportional response is quickly lost. Then, only a spectacle remains.

Some observers fearfully predict that public shaming discourages free expression of ideas and stifles open debate. The so-called "echo chamber" aspect of the internet means that opinions are generally shared only among like-minded communities. If an individual is subject to shaming for expressing views unpopular to an opposing audience, the result will be a more polarized public with more entrenched and uncompromising ideals. This is damaging for political culture and basic civility as well.

So when is shaming appropriate? Many commentators we'll hear from make important distinctions between individuals and institutions, those with power and those without. The basic premise is that when powerful institutions damage the public good, they should be shamed. After all, an institution does not *feel* shame like a person does. Moreover, a corporation is in a position to actually change policies and improve real world conditions. By contrast, it is unlikely that shaming one solitary racist will do much to eradicate racism, regardless of the repugnance of such views.

| *"Fundamentally, the trend in shaming reflects a misunderstanding of the power of social media."*

The Digital Age Amplifies the Dangers of Public Shaming

Kristine Iannelli

In the following viewpoint, Kristine Iannelli recounts the story of Justine Sacco, a public relations professional who was publically shamed for an inappropriate tweet. Sacco was fired from her job and shunned by friends and family for a joke that, however unfunny and insensitive, was arguably taken out of context. Iannelli cites a few studies of how the digital age has changed journalism. According to observers, the internet provides the least powerful in society with a loud platform. However, it also enables this platform to be used irresponsibly. Iannelli equates the needless "calling out" of individuals with bullying. Kristine Iannelli wrote this piece for a class at the University of Delaware. It was nominated by her peers to be published on the Huffington Post.

"Public Shaming on the Internet," Kristine Iannelli, *Huffington Post,* March 11, 2015. Retrieved May 11, 2015. Reprinted by permission.

As you read, consider the following questions:

1. Why was Justine Sacco fired from her job?
2. What might one gain from the online public shaming of a stranger?
3. Why does the author equate digital public shaming with bullying?

"Going to Africa. Hope I don't get AIDS. Just kidding. I'm white!"

Justine Sacco, 30 years old, published the tweet that would destroy her public image on December 20th of 2013, as she was about to board a plane from London to South Africa. She refreshed her feed periodically while she waited to board, but didn't get any replies—not surprising, as she had only 170 followers at the time. The flight from Heathrow took about 11 hours, and when she got cell service back upon her arrival in South Africa, she was shocked. Her career and her personal life were in shambles; she had been digitally shamed.

Sacco, the senior director of corporate communications at media conglomerate IAC, was terminated from her position at the firm before her plane even landed in Cape Town. Her family in South Africa, fervent supporters of the African National Congress party, told her that she had disgraced them on both a personal and political level; her friends were embarrassed to be connected with her.

Sam Biddle of Gawker was anonymously tipped off to Sacco's inelegant tweet and retweeted it to his 15,000 followers, as well as publishing it on his Gawker blog—the ironic headline, "And Now, a Funny Holiday Tweet from IAC's PR Boss."

The urge to shame her publicly was too tantalizing to pass up.

Public shaming is a natural human urge. It was a common form of punishment in early America in the 18th and 19th centuries and was slowly phased out in most states around 1900. Delaware, for reference, kept the pillory until 1905 and public whippings until 1972. The Internet's ubiquity makes it a perfect vehicle for public shaming, though, and destroying a life and a career becomes as easy as pushing a button and exposing an ill-considered message to masses of angry hordes. Moreover, those who start the wave of shaming have an actual incentive to do so—they gain popularity and standing in the digital community, see exponential Klout growth, and expand their base of followers dramatically.

Simon Mainwaring's *We First* includes the charmingly optimistic sentiment that "enabled by the Internet and social media, we are... awakening our innate capacity for empathy" (2001). But the Internet, and social media in particular, have exhibited an alarming tendency to do just the opposite. In the 11 hours while Sacco was in the air between London and Cape Town, #HasJustineLandedYet trended on Twitter and she became an international laughingstock. The Internet offers a largely anonymous venue for users to decontextualize others' idiotic comments and then villainize them.

This idea, that individuals can wield an enormous level of power in informing and exposing the lives of others, is reflected in Clay Shirky's 2009 chapter, "Everyone is a Media Outlet," from *Here Comes Everybody: The Power of Organizing without Organization*. Here, Shirky decries the rise of Web blogs and the "mass amateurization" of news dissemination. No longer are journalists and news organization held to a certain standard of professionalism he argues; the flood of social media exposés means that the most important thing is to be first to see the opportunity for destruction... and pounce.

This mass amateurization is directly linked to the trend of social media shaming. Fundamentally, the trend in shaming reflects a misunderstanding of the power of social media. Even a person with 170 Twitter followers can end up reaching hundreds of thousands if retweeted by the right media personality. Even a person with just 15,000 Twitter followers can ruin another's career. If every amateur social justice warrior on the Internet were held to the journalistic standards that Shirky espouses, we might see a great deal more of Mainwaring's idea of the human "innate capacity for empathy."

Digital shaming is, at best, a reflection of the voice and power that social media has given to the disenfranchised. It takes a low level of privilege and digital literacy to be able to publish a tweet; individuals who would usually be silenced by the established power structure can publicize injustices that may otherwise have gone unnoticed. At the same time, it can be a weapon of digital destruction, capable of torpedoing a person's entire life in a matter of hours.

Justine Sacco's story has an ironic end. About a year later, the Gawker writer who had initially retweeted her and started the conflagration of her career posted an insensitive message of his own on the internet ("Bring Back Bullying") and then, not so long after, a blog post about what he gained from being internet shamed and how he regrets his treatment of Miss Sacco.

In an age when interpersonal communication is primarily driven by digital technology, it is indisputable that bullying is already back—and that it has taken the form of digital public shaming.

> "*Online shaming, conducted via the blogosphere and our burgeoning array of social networking services, creates an environment of surveillance, fear and conformity.*"

Public Shaming Erodes Free Expression

Russell Blackford

In the following viewpoint, Russell Blackford traces the rise of public shaming in the digital age. Blackford notes that free exchange of ideas and criticism of divergent opinions is a pillar of liberal society. Conversely, the rush to shame a private individual who expresses unpopular or even offensive views risks impoverishing our public culture. If people fear "call-outs," they will be more likely to espouse only mainstream views. However, Blackford does draw a distinction between the public shaming of relatively powerless individuals and holding those with a broad platform accountable for unnecessary personal attacks. Russell Blackford is conjoint lecturer in philosophy at the University of Newcastle.

As you read, consider the following questions:

1. What are some characteristics of our new "call-out" culture, according to the author?
2. Does the author think there are cases where some kind of shaming is appropriate?
3. How does the author differentiate between shaming a private individual on one hand, and mainstream media shaming on the other?

Public shaming is not new. It's been used as a punishment in all societies—often embraced by the formal law and always available for day-to-day policing of moral norms. However, over the past couple of centuries, Western countries have moved away from more formal kinds of shaming, partly in recognition of its cruelty.

Even in less formal settings, shaming individuals in front of their peers is now widely regarded as unacceptable behaviour. This signifies an improvement in the moral milieu, but its effect is being offset by the rise of social media and, with it, new kinds of shaming.

Indeed, as Welsh journalist and documentary maker Jon Ronson portrays vividly in his latest book, social media shaming has become a social menace. Ronson's *So You've Been Publicly Shamed* (Picador, 2015) is a timely contribution to the public understanding of an emotionally charged topic.

Shaming is on the rise. We've shifted—much of the time—to a mode of scrutinising each other for purity. Very often, we punish decent people for small transgressions or for no real transgressions at all. Online shaming, conducted via the blogosphere and our burgeoning array of social networking services, creates an environment of surveillance, fear and conformity.

The making of a call-out culture

I noticed the trend—and began to talk about it—around five years ago. I'd become increasingly aware of cases where people with access to large social media platforms used them to "call out" and publicly vilify individuals who'd done little or nothing wrong. Few onlookers were prepared to support the victims. Instead, many piled on with glee (perhaps to signal their own moral purity; perhaps, in part, for the sheer thrill of the hunt).

Since then, the trend to an online call-out culture has continued and even intensified, but something changed during 2015. Mainstream journalists and public intellectuals finally began to express their unease.

There's no sign that the new call-out culture is fading away, but it's become a recognised phenomenon. It is now being discussed more openly, and it's increasingly questioned. That's partly because even its participants—people who assumed it would never happen to *them*—sometimes find themselves "called out" for revealing some impurity of thought. It's become clear that no moral or political affiliation holds patents on the weaponry of shaming, and no one is immune to its effects.

As Ronson acknowledges, he has, himself, taken part in public shamings, though the most dramatic episode was a desperate act of self-defence when a small group of edgy academics hijacked his Twitter identity to make some theoretical point. Shame on them! I don't know what else he could have done to make them back down.

That, however, was an extreme and peculiar case. It involved ongoing abuse of one individual by others who refused to "get" what they were doing to distress him, even when asked to stop. Fascinating though the example is, it is hardly a precedent for handling more common situations.

At one time, if we go along with Ronson, it felt liberating to speak back in solidarity against the voices of politicians, corporate moguls, religious leaders, radio shock jocks, newspaper columnists and others with real power or social influence.

But there can be a slippery slope... from talking back in legitimate ways against, say, a powerful journalist (criticising her views and arguments, and any abusive conduct), to pushing back in less legitimate ways (such as attempting to silence her viewpoint by trying to get her fired), to destroying relatively powerless individuals who have done nothing seriously wrong.

Slippery slope arguments have a deservedly bad reputation. But some slopes really are slippery, and some slippery slope arguments really are cogent. With public online shaming, we've found ourselves, lately, on an especially slippery slope. In more ways than one, we need to get a grip.

Shaming the shamers

Ronson joined in a campaign of social media shaming in October 2009: one that led to some major advertisers distancing themselves from the*Daily Mail* in the UK. This case illustrates some problems when we discuss social media shaming, so I'll give it more analysis than Ronson does.

One problem is that, as frequently happens, it was a case of "shame the shamer." The recipient of the shaming was especially unsympathetic because she was herself a public shamer of others.

The drama followed a distasteful—to say the least—column by Jan Moir, a British journalist with a deplorable modus operandi. Moir's topic was the death of Stephen Gately, one of the singers from the popular Irish band Boyzone.

Gately had been found dead while on holiday in Mallorca with his civil partner, Andrew Cowles. Although the coroner attributed the death to natural causes, Moir wrote that it was "not, by any yardstick, a natural one" and that "it strikes another blow to the happy-ever-after myth of civil partnerships."

Ronson does not make the point explicit in *So You've Been Publicly Shamed*, but what immediately strikes me is that Moir was engaging in some (not-so-)good old-fashioned *mainstream* media shaming. She used her large public platform to hold up identified individuals to be shamed over very private behaviour. Gately could not, of course, feel any shame from beyond the grave, but Moir's column was grossly tasteless since he had not even been buried when it first appeared.

Moir stated, self-righteously: "It is important that the truth comes out about the exact circumstances of [Gately's] strange and lonely death." But *why* was it so important that the public be told such particulars as whether or not Cowles (at least) hooked up that tragic evening for sex with a student whom Moir names, and whether or not some, or all, of the three young men involved used cannabis or other recreational drugs that night?

To confirm Moir's propensities as a public shamer, no one need go further than the same column. She follows her small-minded paragraphs about Gately with a few others that shame "socialite" Tara Palmer-Tomkinson for no worse sin than wearing a revealing outfit to a high-society party.

You get the picture, I trust. I'm not asking that Moir, or anyone else, walk on eggshells lest her language accidentally offend somebody, or prove open to unexpectedly uncharitable interpretations. Quite the opposite: we should all be able to speak with some spontaneity, without constantly censoring how we formulate our thoughts. I'll gladly extend that freedom to Moir.

But Moir is not merely *unguarded* in her language: she can be positively reckless, as with her suggestion that Palmer-Tomkinson's wispy outfit might more appropriately be worn by "Timmy the Tranny, the hat-check personage down at the My-Oh-My supper club in Brighton." No amount of charitable interpretation can prevent the impression that she is often deliberately, or at best uncaringly, hurtful. In those circumstances, I have no sympathy for her if she receives widespread and severe criticism for what she writes.

When it comes to something like Moir's hatchet job on Gately and Cowles, and their relationship, I can understand the urge to retaliate—to shame and punish in return. It's no wonder, then, that Ronson discusses the feeling of empowerment when numerous people, armed with their social media accounts, turned on badly behaved "giants" such as the *Daily Mail* and its contributors. As it seemed to Ronson in those days, not so long ago, "the silenced were getting a voice."

But let's be careful about this.

Some distinctions

A few aspects need to be teased out. Even when responding to the shamers, we ought to think about what's appropriate.

For a start, I am—I'm well aware—being highly critical of Moir's column and her approach to journalism. In that sense, I could be said to be "shaming" her. But we don't have to be utterly silent when confronted by unpleasant behaviour from public figures.

My criticisms are, I submit, fair comment on material that was (deliberately and effectively) disseminated widely to the public. In writing for a large audience in the way she does—especially when she takes an aggressive and hurtful approach toward named individuals—Moir has to expect some push-back.

We can draw reasonable distinctions. I have no wish to go further than *criticism* of what Moir actually said and did. I don't, for example, want to misrepresent her if I can avoid it, to make false accusations, or to punish her in any way that goes beyond criticism. I wouldn't demand that she be no-platformed from a planned event or that advertisers withdraw their money from the *Daily Mail* until she is fired.

The word *criticism* is important. We need to think about when public criticism is fair and fitting, when it becomes disproportionate, and when it spirals down into something mean and brutal.

Furthermore, we can distinguish between 1) Moir's behaviour toward individuals and 2) her views on issues of general importance, however wrong or ugly those views might be. In her 2009 comments on Gately's death, the two are entangled, but it doesn't follow that they merit just the same kind of response.

Moir's column intrudes on individuals' privacy and holds them up for shaming, but it also expresses an opinion on legal recognition of same-sex couples in the form of civil unions. Although she is vague, Moir seems to think that individuals involved in legally recognised same-sex relationships are less likely to be monogamous (and perhaps more likely to use drugs) than people in heterosexual marriages. This means, she seems to imply, that there's something wrong with, or inferior about, same-sex civil unions.

In fairness, Moir later issued an apology in which she explained her view: "I was suggesting that civil partnerships—the introduction of which I am on the record in supporting—have proved just to be as problematic as marriages." This is, however, difficult to square with the words of her original column, where she appears to deny, point blank, that civil unions "are just the same as heterosexual marriages."

Even if she is factually correct about statistical differences between heterosexual marriages and civil unions, this at least doesn't seem to be relevant to public policy. After all, plenty of marriages between straight people are "open" (and may or may not involve the use of recreational drugs), but they are still legally valid marriages.

If someone does think certain statistical facts about civil unions are socially relevant, however, it's always available to them to argue why. They should be allowed to do so without their speech being legally or socially suppressed. It's likewise open to them to produce whatever reliable data might be available. Furthermore, we can't expect critics of civil unions to present their full case on every occasion when they speak up to express a view. That would be an excessive condition for any of us to have to meet when we express ourselves on important topics.

More generally, we can criticise bad ideas and arguments—or even make fun of them if we think they're *that* bad—but as a rule we shouldn't try to stop their expression.

Perhaps some data exists to support Moir's rather sneering claims about civil unions. But an anecdote about the private lives of a particular gay couple proves nothing one way or the other. Once again, many heterosexual marriages are not monogamous, but a sensational story involving a particular straight couple would prove nothing about *how* many.

In short, Moir is entitled to express her jaundiced views about civil unions or same-sex relationships more generally, and the worst she should face is strong criticism, or a degree of satire, aimed primarily at the views themselves. But shining a spotlight on Cowles and Gately was unfair, callous, nasty, gratuitous, and (to use one of her own pet words) sleazy. In addition to criticising her apparent views, we can object strongly when she publicly shames individuals.

Surfing down the slippery slope

Ronson discusses a wide range of cases, and an evident problem is that they can vary greatly, making it difficult to draw overall conclusions or to frame exact principles.

Some individuals who've been publicly shamed clearly enough "started it," but even they can suffer from a cruel and disproportionate backlash. Some have been public figures who've genuinely done something wrong, as with Jonah Lehrer, a journalist who fabricated quotes to make his stories appear more impressive. It's only to be expected that Lehrer's irresponsibility and poor ethics would damage his career. But even in his case, the shaming process was over the top. Some of it was almost sadistic.

Other victims of public shaming are more innocent than Lehrer. Prominent among them is Justine Sacco, whom Ronson views with understandable sympathy. Sacco's career and personal life were ruined after she made an ill-advised tweet on 20 January 2013. It said: "Going to Africa. Hope I don't get AIDS. Just kidding. I'm white!" She was then subjected to an extraordinarily viral Twitter attack that led quickly to her losing her job and becoming an international laughing stock.

It appears that her tweet went viral after a Gawker journalist retweeted it (in a hostile way) to his 15,000 followers at the time— after just one person among Sacco's 170 followers had passed it on to him.

Doxxing

The trend of exposing a person's personal information online, opening a window for criticism and harassment, is a relatively new form of social punishment used against individuals who've demonstrated reprehensible behavior, whether on the internet or in real life.

Some examples of public shaming include Anonymous' hacking of the Westboro Baptist Church's website, releasing the names and personal details online of every member in response to their plan to protest at the funerals of children killed in Sandy Hook. Also by Anonymous, the release of information about students involved in the gang rape of a young girl in Steubenville Ohio.

It has been argued that in most cases those being publicly shamed deserve it, and that this is a consequence is perfectly appropriate for socially deplorable actions. Other arguments state that public shaming does nothing to drive social progress, as a means to please the crowd rather than reform the wrongdoer.

At any rate, it is increasingly obvious that the internet, as a behemoth community, is not something anyone wants pitted against them. Shamed users may have to deal with backlash for a long time due to the permanency of the web. Then again, their actions made this possible.

"Public Shaming: Don't Be on the Receiving End," Jennifer Markert, Curiousmatic, August 22, 2013.

Ronson offers his own interpretation of the Sacco tweet:

> It seemed obvious that her tweet, whilst not a great joke, wasn't racist, but a self-reflexive comment on white privilege—on our tendency to naively imagine ourselves immune to life's horrors. Wasn't it?

In truth, it's *not* obvious to me just how to interpret the tweet, and of course I can't read Sacco's mind. If it comes to that, I doubt that she pondered the wording carefully. Still, this small piece of sick humour was aimed only at her small circle of Twitter followers, and it probably did convey to them something along the lines of what Ronson suggests. In its original context, then, it did not merely ridicule the plight of black AIDS victims in Africa.

Much satire and humour is, as we know, unstable in its meaning—simultaneously saying something outrageous and testing our emotions as we find ourselves laughing at it. It can make us squirm with uncertainty. This applies (sometimes) to high literary satire, but also to much ordinary banter among friends. We laugh but we also squirm.

In any event, charitable interpretations—if not a single straightforward one—were plainly available for Sacco's tweet. This was a markedly different situation from Jan Moir's gossip-column attacks on hapless celebrities and socialites. And unlike Moir, Sacco lacked a large media platform, an existing public following, and an understanding employer.

Ronson also describes the case of Lindsey Stone, a young woman whose life was turned to wreckage because of a photograph taken in Arlington National Cemetery in Virginia. In the photo she is mocking a "Silence and Respect" sign by miming a shout and making an obscene gesture. The photo was uploaded on Facebook, evidently with inadequate privacy safeguards, and eventually it went viral, with Stone being attacked by a cybermob coming from a political direction opposite to the mob that went after Sacco.

While the Arlington photograph might seem childish, or many other things, posing for it and posting it on Facebook hardly add up to any serious wrongdoing. It is not behaviour that merited the outcome for Lindsey Stone: destruction of her reputation, loss of her job, and a life of ongoing humiliation and fear.

Referring to such cases, Ronson says:

> The people we were destroying were no longer just people like Jonah [Lehrer]: public figures who had committed actual transgressions. They were private individuals who really hadn't done anything much wrong. Ordinary humans were being forced to learn damage control, like corporations that had committed PR disasters.

Thanks to Ronson's intervention, Stone sought help from an agency that rehabilitates online reputations. Of Stone's problems in particular, he observes:

> The sad thing was that Lindsey had incurred the Internet's wrath because she was impudent and playful and foolhardy and outspoken. And now here she was, working with Farukh [an operative for the rehabilitation agency] to reduce herself to safe banalities—to cats and ice cream and Top 40 chart music. We were creating a world where the smartest way to survive is to be bland.

This is not the culture we wanted

Ronson also quotes Michael Fertik, from the agency that helped Stone: "We're creating a culture where people feel constantly surveilled, where people are afraid to be themselves."

"We see ourselves as nonconformist," Ronson concludes sadly, "but I think all of this is creating a more conformist, conservative age."

This is not the culture we wanted. It's a public culture that seems broken, but what can we do about it?

For a start, it helps to recognise the problem, but it's difficult, evidently, for most people to accept the obvious advice: Be forthright in debating topics of general importance, but always subject to some charity and restraint in how you treat particular people. Think through—and not with excuses—what that means in new situations. Be willing to criticise people on your own side if they are being cruel or unfair.

It's not our job to punish individuals, make examples of them, or suppress their views. Usually we can support our points without any of this; we can do so in ways that are kinder, more honest, more likely to make intellectual progress. The catch is, it requires patience and courage.

Our public culture needs more of this sort of patience, more of this sort of courage. Can we—will we—rise to the challenge?

> "*Unchecked outrage—comprising only of scorn—which so often results from publicly shaming, is unhelpful, if not a hindrance.*"

Public Shaming Disrupts Due Process

Tauriq Moosa

In the following viewpoint, Tauriq Moosa argues that public shaming too often violates the principle of proportionality. In other words, the severity of public shaming as a punishment is very often unsuitable for the transgressions in question, which are often quite minor. Sometimes, shaming achieves a critical mass when the person being shamed hasn't done anything. Moosa argues that this is a dangerous form of mob justice that relies more on gut feelings than due process and truth. Tauriq Moosa is a tutor in ethics, bioethics, and critical thinking at the University of Cape Town in South Africa.

As you read, consider the following questions:

1. What problems does the author identify with public shaming?
2. Why might celebrities be vulnerable to internet shaming? Are they more equipped to handle it?
3. How does the author recommend we deal with our moral outrage?

"The Dangers of Public Shaming, Mob Justice and Scolding on the Internet," Tauriq Moosa, *New Statesman*, January 29, 2014. Reprinted by permission.

E ven when people are obviously wrong, is shaming them on the internet a good way to improve the world?

Whether it's a woman issuing a racist tweet heard around the world; bigots judging a woman's abilities, whether as a sportsperson or journalist, on her looks; an irritable (but evidently non-existent) fellow passenger on a plane; men making silly sexist comments at a tech convention; high school students making racist remarks about Obama's re-election—all were targets of public shaming through digital media, most predominantly social. It's both tempting and easy to shame such people with modern digital platforms (a retweet, capturing and storing screenshots, etc). But even when such people are so obviously morally wrong, we must question the efficacy of public shaming—as a form of response.

That it's easy to use social media for public shaming isn't enough reason to do so. Bigger questions are at stake: proportionality is an essential factor in trying to redress wrongs, since we don't get moral immunity for being morally right. Shooting someone who takes your parking space, for example, isn't right just because the thief was wrong.

Wrongs shouldn't go unpunished, of course, and just because we should question the practice of public shaming doesn't mean we never respond to wrong or bad behaviour at all; it only means we should act wiser and better—it means reflecting on whether initiating or participating in public shaming is actually a good option.

There appear to be two major problems with public shaming.

Problem 1: Public shaming becomes—and/ or is—another name for mob justice

With digital platforms and followers, pointing at something can be the same as shooting a magic spell made of an outraged audience.

Let's take a fairly innocuous but very public example. After Nelson Mandela's death, an alleged Paris Hilton tweet was retweeted and posted and mocked widely. Supposedly, Hilton thanked Mandela for writing the "I have a dream" speech. People quickly informed Ms Hilton that she was all kinds of idiot, all kinds of female anatomy parts, all kinds of waste product.

Annoyingly for the name-callers (including the prestigious Foreign Policy), there is no evidence to suppose Hilton ever sent such a tweet. But to those doing the shaming, did it really matter? All that mattered was a reason to deride, to hate, to show how much better and smarter these people were than a "dumb reality show star."

We are better than her.

By displaying examples of racism or sexism or other forms of bigotry; by showing kids who mock Olympic athletes or any of the people listed in the first paragraph; our public shaming invites us to form a conglomerate of the morally righteous to beat these people with our Ethics Sticks. We respond sometimes with even worse messages—expletives, namecalling and threats—than what was initially articulated. But no hypocrisy is noticed because we, after all, are morally right and we can, therefore, do no wrong. Just look how many others are doing it, too!

If you think you have moral immunity in how you respond to an act you deem wrong, if you're bolstered by witnessing mutual reaction and views from others to the wrong act, this is essentially mob justice.

And mob justice is not, in fact, justice due to the inherent unfairness.

Taken together, those "accusing" have voices which vastly overpower the accused, meaning that there is no way for Hilton to respond to the accusation. In the case above, when she and others pointed out that she hadn't sent the tweet, few people corrected themselves.

It is an essential feature of modern law to presume innocence and give an accused individual the ability to respond on an equal platform to allegations of wrongdoing. But this cannot be the case when everyone is more interested in laughing at and mocking and threatening an alleged wrongdoer than in assessing whether the wrongdoer is actually guilty.

Problem 2: No regulation, no middle ground, no persons

Mob justice's worrying element then is precisely that the "accusers" are also the judges, the juries, the executioners: there is no one "above" the group. The idea of a defence is unknown, there is only someone to be punished by shaming.

This inability to respond should worry all of us. Celebrities at least have professional managers and PR firms, who can work round the clock; they have secure enough incomes that, even after such public mishaps, they won't be destitute.

But for us mortals, we have no such luxury.

If you are some unknown person who is terrible at making crude jokes, anyone can decide to target you for shaming. Including Buzzfeed reporters with over 100,000 Twitter followers. Many of us don't have the million-dollar lawyers and PR firm to help us respond: we're one person, fighting down the voices of the self-righteous many.

When I pointed out that Justine Sacco was a target of hate, many emailed expressing dismay that I would compare Sacco to other bullying victims. "She deserved everything she got!" I was told. Her tweet made her deserving of death and rape threats, of being followed and tracked, of being photographed by a stranger? They claimed yes: because "She was wrong," remember, and they were right.

Apparently, there can be no mistakes on the internet, made by a fallible human, with emotions and spur-of-the-moment responses. Either you're with them or against them. This is the digital mob and its form of punishment can turn on anyone: no matter how famous; no matter how deserving. Proportionality is as important as truth—in other words, somewhat irrelevant.

This should be worrying to all of us, even if we're not racists, homophobes or other kinds of bigots.

We forget that, by definition, platforms of all kinds create a caricature of the user. There are no Sauron-like villains, emitting evil and hate—it's human being, people with failures and loves and hates and passions and families and friends. Yet, we see a single tweet and judge them; we see a single blogpost and determine his or her entire worth.

There's no need to be a racist to see that wanting an alleged racist to be raped is wrong: we're still dealing with people, not a picture on your monitor. With no bigger authority, there is no way to direct this outrage in ways that might actually be beneficial, to call a halt to furious cries. Consider, for example, how during the outrage of Justine Sacco, someone bought a domain with her name and redirected it to an Aids charity. In one swoop, it showed the idiocy of Sacco's tweet and got people to channel their rage into a beneficial direction. This didn't just say "Look at this dumb racist!" and let slip the pugs of outrage.

Whither our outrage?

None of this means outrage is bad. It just means unchecked outrage—comprising only of scorn—which so often results from publicly shaming, is unhelpful, if not a hindrance. There are better ways to respond than knee-jerk anger, even if the other person is wrong (or you're told he's wrong by someone you regard as an authority.)

Being morally right is not enough. We must be able to convey that morally: responding to a racist with a snarky joke or thoughtful blogpost is miles away from responding with a fist. Responses don't have the same moral weight just because the responses are defending a (proper) moral position.

And public shaming, as we've noted, is highly problematic: there is no encouragement to ascertain truth (Hilton didn't confuse Dr King and Mandela, but who cares?); no dialogue is created, only a target painted on someone's back. Even if you abhor threats, you can't control all people's reactions nor who will see your tweet, your Facebook post, your photo of the racist, sexist, etc. And, even if someone did make a public fool of himself, it's hard to support the pile-on of threats and responses when it takes a serious toll on actual people's lives, when there's little evidence his bad behaviour significantly harmed anyone. There will always be people who hold stupid beliefs, but public shaming doesn't seem like a moral way to respond when it's dependent on an unregulated "public."

Are we silent on racism? Of course not. Nor are we silent about sexism or other forms of bigotry, just because we don't publicly shame. There are many ways to respond and, if we genuinely care about combating bigotry and stupidity, we must assess whether our responses are themselves helpful to the cause.

Again, just because you're responding to racism or sexism doesn't make your response right. I've seen no good come of publicly shaming someone, when public shaming is the sole response. Sure, someone is also shamed after being rightfully convicted, fired, etc, but there "justice" wasn't merely a retweet.

(Digital) public shaming as the sole method of response, in terms of justice, should not be implemented. As perhaps a by-product of other kinds of justified responses, we may support it. However, I am still hesitant and, if I wish to highlight terrible beliefs or views, I default to anonymise the person (as much as possible), when using social media.

When there can be an equality of platform, like say blogs or columns, this becomes irrelevant—but there, inherent unfairness is potentially undermined (and it's not about just threatening the other person!).

We must remember that, even though they may act bigoted, we're still dealing with people, who have friends, family and loved ones; we must remember that combating bigotry takes on a moral dimension not only in terms of beliefs but responses.

| "*Your time would be much better spent wagging a finger at the 90 companies responsible for the bulk of historical emissions.*"

Institutions and Corporations That Do Harm Should Be Shamed

Amelia Urry

In the following viewpoint, the author summarizes an interview with author Jennifer Jacquet. In her book Is Shame Necessary? New Uses for an Old Tool, *Jacquet makes distinctions that are useful in navigating affective emotions such as shame and guilt, recasting the former as valuable. While guilt unproductively shifts attention to individuals, shame can influence institutions and corporations that actively harm the environment. Jacquet is critical of our consumerist paradigm that assigns too much responsibility to individuals. Instead, we should expose and shame those on the production side who engage in irresponsible and environmentally degrading practices. Amelia Urry is Grist's associate editor of science and technology, and self-appointed poet-in-residence.*

"Does Shame Have a Place in the Climate Fight? Jennifer Jacquet Thinks So," Amelia Urry, Grist.org, June 26, 2015. Reprinted by permission.

As you read, consider the following questions:

1. What is the difference between guilt and shame according to Jacquet?
2. Where is the "sweet spot" of shame?
3. How does Jacquet define soft power?

J ennifer Jacquet thinks we all need more shame in our lives.

At least, that's the premise of her pointedly titled book *Is Shame Necessary?: New Uses for an Old Tool,* in which she describes the troubling lack of chagrin demonstrated by the corporations and governments that have been busily trashing the environment for decades, nay, centuries. Meanwhile, the more sensitive among us (i.e. anyone who has ever Asked Umbra) are wracked with guilt about what untold horrors our lint rollers and beach reads and unweeded gardens might wreak on the climate.

To roughly paraphrase Jacquet: Chill, y'all! No one is going to make or break the planet on one anxiety-ridden trip to Whole Foods, so stop acting like it. Your time would be much better spent wagging a finger at the 90 companies responsible for the bulk of historical emissions.

We sat down with Jacquet to talk about the difference between guilt and shame, and why the latter will serve us much better than the former. Along the way, we stumbled across some other vocab terms, and she was happy to tell us all about them. No need to crack a dictionary this time, folks—we've got your climate shame glossary right here.

This interview has been edited and condensed.

Guilt vs. Shame

"For me, guilt is about an internal conversation you have with yourself, about your own moral standards and how you hold yourself to those. Whereas shame, the way I define it, means thinking about what others think about you, or concerning yourself with the way that others think about you."

"The fundamental way in which guilt has risen in our society is through a very subtle but profound shift in focusing our attention from supply, and the way industries operate, to focusing on the demand side. That puts a lot of so-called decisions in the hands of consumers, individuals. So pesticide use or battery-raised hens or animal cruelty more broadly [or] unfair trade—this is now something that each and every one of us is asked to feel guilty about, because what we buy is contributing."

"You can arguably shame people who are shameless, in a strange way, as long as you expose them to public opprobrium. Even if they don't feel shame—and it's very likely they may not—do they change their behavior in response to the stimuli, even if they don't feel a certain way?"

Moral Licensing

"This is what happens when, if you somehow do something positive in one domain, it leads to negative behavior in another. If I buy an eco-certified product, maybe later I'll justify taking a flight—something with much higher marginal impacts."

The Attention Economy

"We don't live in the information age, we live in an attention age—information is not scarce, attention is. And everybody in marketing knows this—but shame, like marketing, is only as good as the number of people involved, or the power of the eyeballs involved."

"There's a lot of strategy going on behind actually getting attention. Maybe in some cases—let's say, the latest political scandal—you don't have to try much at all. But as most of us know who do any environmental or labor or animal issues, people are quite tapped out. So shaming—or social change in general—has to reach out to the arts, and to the people who are really in the business of getting attention."

SHAMING FOR THE GOOD

Some recent cases of shaming show us how social disapproval might be wielded in considerate and effective ways. Non-profit groups, including Netherlands-based BankTrack, have spent the last five years calling out the worst banks funding mountaintop-removal coal mining in Appalachia, which is environmentally destructive but not yet illegal. After being exposed, several banks vowed to phase out their relationship with mountaintop removal, thus demonstrating the power of shame to work at large scales.

Several studies, including one my colleagues and I conducted, have shown that singling out bad apples in social dilemmas can lead to greater co-operation. Polls show that the vast majority of Americans, including half of Republicans, believe we should take action on climate change, but members of Congress block legislation. Recently, non-profit group Organizing for Action made it easy to call out climate denialists in the US Congress privately over email or publicly over Twitter, and even hosted a climate-change fantasy tournament between the 16 worst climate denialists in Congress.

Digital technologies have made it possible for each of us to instigate online shaming—and each potentially become its victim—but more important, we are now asked every day which issues matter enough to weigh in on. Given the limited nature of attention, and how essential attention is to shaming's effectiveness, we must ask ourselves which issues to prioritise. We might share concerns about a shame-filled world that leads to individual suffering and worry that punishment online is disproportionate and lacks due process. But shaming, aimed well, cautiously and at the right time, can improve society.

"Public Shaming Makes the World a Better Place?" Jennifer Jacquet, *Wired* magazine, August 2015.

#TheBlackfishEffect

"Since the Blackfish film was released, the stock value of SeaWorld has dropped 60 percent, which is enormous, even though attendance has only fallen 5 percent. Why is that? Maybe it's the right film at the right time. But there might be more specific reasons—think about Food Inc., where the target is not exactly clear. There are a lot of issues with food! Whereas Blackfish had a very clear and easy—maybe to some degree, oversimplified—target. SeaWorld is not the only corporation doing this, but they're very much the target of the shaming. Plus, there was a human element of 'gosh, this is really putting humans at risks.'"

"This is a perfect storm."

Bullying

"When the strong try to shame the weak." [Editor's note: Not cool.]

The Sweet Spot of Shame

"Does the crowd find it acceptable? Is it actually the weak aiming against the strong? It's not too weak, it's not too strong, it doesn't get [zero] attention, but it doesn't get too much attention. In some ways, people are criticizing climate for trumping every other environmental issue."

"For issues related to the environment, shame is more salient than it might be for others. For example, there's an app that alerts your social network if you press the snooze button too many times in the morning. That's not a great use of shaming, because the audience is not inherently concerned with your transgression. Whereas [with] environmental issues like water pollution—maybe even the disappearance of certain species—these are problems that by their very nature concern all of us. Because they're cooperation dilemmas, because you're doing something that affects my enjoyment or my future, that makes it inherently more of a social dilemma, and therefore lends itself to social tools."

"Almost all environmental issues fall into that. With climate change, while we are all in it together, certain countries are going to pay disproportionate costs. And those countries, conveniently, are not the ones doing the pollution. I think the pervasive unfairness in the problem of climate change is really difficult—that's why those countries have the option of using shame, and have done this really great street theatre. But I think there is way more room for shaming the U.S. and China from these countries than they've picked up on so far."

Humor as a Tool

"Not just humor, per se; it's like *The Onion* or *The Daily Show*—it's humor with an added twist of irony. It's not a knock-knock joke. It's really asking us to engage more actively with something."

[Ed. Note: Here, Jacquet drops a headline from The Onion] "'Dolphins Evolve Opposable Thumbs, Humanity Says "Oh [expletive]."' You get the joke, because you have to understand that dolphins are smarter than humans. That's the whole undercurrent—it's just resting on the surface quite nicely. That's what Jon Stewart does."

Concealed Irony

"If Jon Stewart is pure irony, Colbert is concealed irony — you have to be in on the joke. The question is how well they work; they definitely work to get attention. There are writers — like David Foster Wallace or Jonathan Franzen — who say that sincerity is needed. Some people criticize the climate movement for being a little too earnest, but, on the other hand, attention is not the end goal. The end goal is large-scale changes in behavior. And it may or may not be that concealed irony leads to those outcomes. What's for certain is that it's attention grabbing. Past that, there may have to be some other, more sincere strategy involved."

"Shame on Me? Well, Shame on You."

"When you carry out a shaming campaign, you put yourself at risk of being dragged through the mud as well. Anything else, anything you can find, any dirt on someone you can say, 'Well, you did this.' Then it's a struggle for who has the better reputation."

"Westboro Baptist Church are notorious shamers, very unsuccessfully so. Often they have the effect of moving the dial even further in the direction that they'd hoped to avoid."

"Climategate is another great [Editor's note: she means "terrible"] case of that. That was timed so strategically to be right before Copenhagen. That was a pure PR stunt. The effects were never reversed. Copenhagen ended with zero success — there were nice write-ups, in Nature, but ask your average undergrad and they don't have that impression at all. That was a real number on climate scientists generally."

Rough Justice vs. Soft Power

"Shame can be either of these things. The whole goal is for soft power, not rough justice. Maybe in some cases, harsh is necessary — but that harshness is aimed at institutions that don't leave a bunch of victims in their wake."

"There's that saying 'guns don't kill people, people kill people.' We know that's not necessarily true, right? Shame is like that — it's not exactly value-neutral. It's designed to do harm. But there can be moments in which it can really work as a positive force in society. My point with the book was to get people to reconsider shame as being simply a negative force."

| "These days, public shaming is our favorite brand of small-batch artisanal justice."

Courts Using Creative Forms of Punishment Should Also Use Caution

Greg Beato

In the following viewpoint, Greg Beato chronicles some of the novel forms of punishment now being meted out by judges across the country. For lesser, nonviolent crimes, many courts are turning to the age-old tactic of shaming perpetrators. Some are required to broadcast their transgressions via signs while others are forced to have special identifying features on their vehicle. These punishments are cheaper than incarceration, but in the digital age, it is impossible to predict the reach of even small punishments. This raises issues of proportionality that are difficult to answer. Greg Beato has written for dozens of publications, including SPIN, Wired, Business 2.0, *and the* San Francisco Chronicle.

"The Shame of Public Shaming," Greg Beato, Reason.com, July 2013 Issue. Reprinted by permission.

As you read, consider the following questions:

1. What are some examples of judges using public shaming as punishment?
2. Why might public shaming be an appealing alternative form of sentencing?
3. According to the author, what makes this form of justice inherently unpredictable?

In America, our justice system is designed to be slow, methodical, a little boring. This is especially true in the sentencing phase. Even-tempered bureaucrats in bland black uniforms consult elaborately detailed guidelines to ensure that punishment is applied in consistent fashion across similar cases.

Occasionally, though, our black-clad functionaries break out of the mold. In November 2012, for example, Cleveland Municipal Judge Pinkey Carr compelled a 32-year-old woman to stand on a street corner for two hours, holding a hastily scribbled sign that said "Only an idiot would drive on the sidewalk to avoid a schoolbus."

The case received tremendous media attention, and apparently Judge Carr was pleased enough with the results to make public shaming a standard part of her repertoire. In March 2013, she sentenced a 58-year-old man who had called 911 and threatened to kill police officers to 90 days in jail, plus a hefty chaser of humiliation. This offender, Carr ruled, would be required to stand outside Cleveland's Second District Police Department building for one week, three hours each day, holding a sign that reads "I was being an idiot and it will never happen again."

Carr's sentencing sentiments are not an anomaly. These days, public shaming is our favorite brand of small-batch artisanal justice. Evoking the authentic no-nonsense morality of our Puritan forebears, while also seeming quirky and novel, creative punishment is what today's most discerning consumers of hand-crafted, state-sanctioned vengeance demand.

Last year, the National Institute of Justice released a report showing that in 59 percent of the 826 cities included in its study, police departments, local media outlets, and other parties publicize the identities of prostitution clients, often before they've been convicted of a crime. In Arlington, Texas, the preferred delivery system for disgrace is a highway billboard. In Fresno, California, the police department maintains a webpage it calls "Operation Reveal," where it posts photos of individuals who've been arrested on prostitution-related charges.

In Ohio, if you're convicted of drunk driving, you may be required to place a bright yellow license plate on your car. In January 2013, Montana legislators introduced a bill that would mandate orange plates for people with a DUI conviction. "Those in favor of the bill say people with DUI's need to be put on display so they can be embarrassed by their crime," a local ABC affiliate, KFBB, reported on its newscast.

The public, too, loves public shaming. Landlords take to Craigslist to complain about tenants who haven't paid rent. Outraged deliverymen post photographs of miserly tippers on their Tumblr sites. Jilted maître d's tweet the names of customers who bailed on their reservations. Frustrated pug owners humiliate serial carpet-poopers at dogshaming.com.

In 1979, when New York City Mayor Ed Koch ordered radio station WNYC, then owned by the city, to broadcast the names of nine men convicted of soliciting prostitutes, an unsigned *New York Times* editorial described his actions as a "mighty misuse of government power." In another article, *Times* columnist William Safire dubbed Koch the "Mayatollah," and chastised him for "reaching back three centuries" to dredge up this archaic tactic.

But what struck the chattering classes of 1979 as astonishingly regressive seems strikingly commonplace in 2013. As connoisseurs of Malibu mug shots can attest, ceremonial humiliation via electronic media now stands as a widely practiced antidote to celebrity-style above-it-all transgression. Public shaming also takes the most coveted value of our age—publicity—and turns it on its head. Any form of publicity so unpleasant that it qualifies as punishment must be severe indeed, worse even than jail time, house arrest, fines, or community service.

Koch's regressive "John Hour" was only slightly ahead of its time. Though it lasted just one episode, and that episode undersold its title by about 58 minutes, the ensuing years produced new green shoots of humiliation across the country.

In 1983, a judge in Fort Bend County, Texas, had 250 red, white, and blue bumper stickers printed up to identify people on probation for driving while intoxicated. By 1985, he'd gone through approximately a third of his supply and judges in Oklahoma and Florida had adopted the practice as well.

In 1984, a judge in Tennessee offered a car thief a chance to avoid incarceration by publicizing his crime for 30 days via a 5'x4' sign posted in his front yard. In 1986, prosecutors in Lincoln County, Oregon, offered plea bargains to nonviolent offenders if they paid for an ad in a local newspaper featuring their mug shot and an apology. "It's somewhat reminiscent, I suppose, of the public stockade, where you were publicly put on display for your indiscretion," a Lincoln County district attorney told a UPI reporter. The intent, the reporter elaborated, was to "bring embarrassment or fear to criminals."

Lincoln County started its public shaming program in part because of a shortage of jail space—it needed a cheaper way to deal with criminals than incarcerating them. In addition to being economical, public shaming is, in many practical ways, a less severe and disruptive form of punishment than being locked up for a given period of time, and thus potentially a good alternative for less serious crimes, especially for first offenders.

But public shaming these days is obviously different than it was in the 1600s, or even the trailblazing 1980s. In an essay that appeared in the Spring 1996 issue of the *University of Chicago Law Review*, the legal scholar Dan Kahan explained how public shaming in early America began to fall out of favor in part because America was becoming more populous and impersonal. "In a society of strangers," Kahan wrote, "the bare deprivation of status no longer resonated as a symbol of the community's moral disapproval."

In a post-1996 society of highly connected social networks and online forums, community moral disapproval is one of the world's most abundant resources. But it's also unpredictable.

In early incarnations, public shaming was a relatively fixed form of punishment. It could be long (you're literally branded with a letter signifying your adulterous transgression), or it could be short (you have to spend 48 hours in the town-square stockade), but either way it was fixed. Punishments were assigned, executed, and then they were over.

Today, public shaming exercises haphazardly mix the real world with virtual reality. Judge Pinkey Carr sentences you to three hours of public sign-holding, but it's impossible to predict how many photos and videos the news media and random passersby may produce. Nor can you predict how much notice this imagery will attract. Maybe it will hit the Web but die with little fanfare. Maybe it will become a viral sensation.

Given that the whole point of public humiliation is to turn attention into punishment, an audience of one million is a more severe punishment than an audience of one thousand. What this means, effectively, is that when a judge orders a person to stand with a sign, or even when a police station publishes the mug shot of a prostitution client, they don't really know what degree of punishment they're sanctioning. The reason that one photograph goes viral and another does not often has nothing to do with the crime being punished, but rather on what the person being punished looks like, or what kind of news day it is, or which particularly influential blogger or tweeter decides to note the case.

Judges have the power to create their own unique sentences. And courts have ruled that sentences involving public shaming are constitutional as long as they aspire to some other goal, such as deterrence or retribution.

But equal application of the law is a crucial element of our justice system. It's one of the reasons we have sentencing guidelines.

And quirky punishments designed to go viral don't just fail to meet this standard of the law; they actively subvert it. Their primary goal is to court publicity, and that publicity can't be accurately anticipated or controlled.

Public shaming may make for good YouTube content. And perhaps it can help end the scourge of restaurant reservation non-compliance. (No studies have been conducted yet measuring its efficacy in this regard.) In the end, though, it's a tool best left to furious maître d's and frustrated pet-owners. The allegedly impartial men and women who oversee our courtroom aren't tasked with meting out novelty and entertainment. They're tasked with meting out justice, and justice works best when it's delivered in uniform, predictable fashion.

Periodical and Internet Sources Bibliography

The following articles have been selected to supplement the diverse views presented in this chapter.

Leland Beaumont, "Humiliation," Emotional Competency, Retrieved September 2016. http://www.emotionalcompetency.com/humiliation.htm.

Robert X. Cringely, "Public Shaming and Internet Bullies on Parade," InfoWorld, April 20, 2015. http://www.infoworld.com/article/2912232/cringely/public-shaming-internet-bullies-on-parade.html.

Donna Navarro, "'Public Shaming' Can Sometimes Be a Force for Good," *Nottingham Post*, October 1, 2015. http://www.nottinghampost.com/donna-navarro-8216-public-shaming-8217-force-good/story-27895420-detail/story.html.

Pablo Ramirez, "Written in Stone: Social Media's Immediacy and Our Online Comments," *Undergraduate Times,* August 22, 2014. http://ugtimes.com/2014/08/opinion/written-in-stone-social-medias-immediacy-and-our-online-comments.

Cole Stryker, "The Problem with Public Shaming," *The Nation*, April 24, 2013. https://www.thenation.com/article/problem-public-shaming.

Joanna Weiss, "Does Public Shaming Work?" *Boston Globe*, April 17, 2014. https://www.bostonglobe.com/opinion/2014/04/17/opextrashame/NqPSPXmvQOK4fXtmLtn8qN/story.html.

CHAPTER 2

Is Public Shaming an Effective Disciplinary Tool?

Chapter Preface

P arents and other authority figures are becoming increasingly
inclined to use shame as a disciplinary tool of late for minors
in their charge. As teens increasingly conduct their social lives
online, parental shaming is now often done through posts on social
media designed to embarrass or otherwise demean as punishment
for problematic behavior. Instead of more traditional punishments
such as grounding, now a parent of a student who brings home a
poor report card might post a picture on Facebook of their child
holding a sign that says, "I need to study more." Is this trend of
online parental shaming effective? More important, does it promote
healthy development for children and adolescents? The articles
in this chapter tackle this question from a few different angles.

Parent still have considerable leeway in how they raise their
children, despite widespread condemnation of spanking and other
kinds of corporal punishments as abuse. This means that if a father
decides to cut his daughter's hair to humiliate her, no one has the
authority to stop this act. How deeply this will affect the girl in
question depends on a number of factors. If the family is close,
the episode may be soon forgotten and even laughed about. If the
family dynamic is tense, such action can weaken communication
and ultimately erode a child's self-confidence. In extreme cases,
it can be a factor in a subsequent suicide. In addition, there is no
way to predict how widely circulated a shame photo may become.
A photo that goes viral can be damaging far beyond the parent's
original intent and the child's transgression.

Race, class, and gender play important roles in how deeply
parental shaming affects the child. The backdrop of racism can
amplify and distort. Focusing on race, the trend of giving young
black children old man "Benjamin Button"–style haircuts plays
into a cultural tendency to "adultify" African American boys. This
potentially places them in harms way from the police, already
prejudiced against black youth. Likewise, shaming may affect girls

more than boys, and the poor more than the wealthy. Thus, a monolithic conclusion on shaming must be avoided.

Teachers have fairly broad control over what happens in their classroom. In some cases, this latitude allows parents and teachers to downplay the potentially damaging effects of shame. Some wonder if singling out a child's behavior in front of their peers can leave that child feeling marginalized. In a group setting, marginalization can undermine the corrective attempt, causing the shamed child to become withdrawn. For this reason, some educational counselors caution against using shame as a disciplinary action in school.

| "*A key aim of the calls to name and shame is addressed at recidivism. This is based on the false assumption that if the names of young offenders could be published or broadcast then this would thwart their criminal careers.*"

Shaming Juvenile Offenders Does Not Benefit Anyone

Robyn Lincoln

In the following viewpoint, Robyn Lincoln argues that the naming of youthful offenders does not benefit—and in fact may harm—the offenders, victims, and society as a whole. Making public the names of juvenile offenders is a form of public shaming, intended to inhibit future infractions. But there is scant evidence that the practice has any such effect. Instead, juveniles involved in criminal proceedings may feel they need to commit additional crimes in order to uphold their reputation. Robyn Lincoln teaches criminology at Bond University and has researched and taught at other universities in southeast Queensland, Australia.

"Naming and Shaming Young Offenders: Reactionary Politicians Are Missing the Point," Robyn Lincoln, *The Conversation*, August 21, 2012. https://theconversation.com/naming-and-shaming-young-offenders-reactionary-politicians-are-missing-the-point-8690. Licensed under CC BY ND 4.0 International.

As you read, consider the following questions:

1. How does the author distinguish positive forms of shaming from those she criticizes?
2. What are the goals of publicly shaming juvenile offenders?
3. Which youth in particular does the author single out as being especially harmed by shaming policies?

L ast month, Queensland's Attorney-General Jarrod Bleijie called for the public naming of all youth who appear in court.

Echoing practices from the deep south of the USA where t-shirts, signs outside homes and photographs of errant teenagers have been used, Queensland has jumped on the "name and shame" bandwagon … and not for the first time.

During the 2006 Queensland election campaign the then-Coalition parties wanted to make it mandatory to name juveniles over 13 years who had committed a serious offence.

Again in 2009 there was political stoushing between Anna Bligh and Lawrence Springborg about identifying delinquent youth.

A nation-wide issue

Queensland is not alone in promulgating name and shame policies. This issue has been raised in New South Wales and more recently in Western Australia.

Similar proposals have emanated from Canada, and were put into practice via civil Anti-Social Behaviour Orders in the United Kingdom under its previous government.

But where is the evidence to suggest that the public identification of juveniles who are involved in criminal proceedings will have a positive effect on their subsequent behaviour? Where is the evidence that such naming will be of benefit to communities or even to victims of crime?

The short answer: there is precious little.

"Good" shaming versus reactionary rhetoric

Recent research has centred on the more positive forms of shaming, which are believed to be a part of restorative justice practices, such as "youth accountability conferences." These programs utilise the positive, transformative power of shaming, while avoiding the negative effects of public stigmatisation.

While apparently politically appealing, cries to openly name and shame are ill-informed.

Politicians pushing for the names of juvenile offenders to be in large bold type in newspapers or, worse still, depicted on broadcast news or captured forever on the internet fail to deal with the stigma attached to these kinds of practices.

The name and shame proposals, apart from ignoring fundamental international principles espoused in documents such as the Convention on the Rights of the Child, also fail to consider which young people might be subject to such naming.

These young people are often from backgrounds of multiple disadvantage, and who may be subject to some form of welfare protection. In these cases, welfare acts often contain provisions that prohibit public disclosure of identities.

So while reactionary politicians seek reform to juvenile justice regulations, they may find that efforts to name and shame will be stymied because young people are under the "care" of their own governments.

It is also the case that those calling the loudest to name and shame offer the caveat that they "only wish to name the really rotten ones" (and I am aware of at least one newspaper editor who invoked this refrain, only he used somewhat "bluer" language).

Presumably then, a key aim of the calls to name and shame is addressed at recidivism. This is based on the false assumption that if the names of young offenders could be published or broadcast then this would thwart their criminal careers.

The reality is that those young people already well-embedded in the juvenile justice system are unlikely to be swayed by naming and shaming.

Parenting in the Digital Age

Social media is not private, even if you post something to a small group of friends. Sharing a humiliating Facebook message, YouTube clip, or Instagram photo of your kids is the same as yelling at them on your front lawn—only multiplied by the global population. You cannot control where your message goes or how many people will view it. Maybe it works sometimes and your kid changes his ways, but I don't think your teen will ever truly get over a humiliation on that grand a scale.

Public shaming is not discipline. It humiliates a young person about a mistake they've made. It doesn't lead to better behaviour—if anything, it probably leads to a decreased sense of self-worth. Dr. Brene Brown has an Oprah-level career writing about the damage that shame causes people. She writes in *The Gifts of Imperfection*, "Shame, blame, disrespect, betrayal, and the withholding of affection damage the roots from which love grows. Love can only survive these injuries if they are acknowledged, healed and rare."

Parenting in the digital age is hard, and our kids understand the Internet a whole lot better than we do. I understand why, in a fit of anger, parents may want to turn the tables and use the power of social media to teach their child a lesson. But it isn't right. Unfortunately, when it comes to discipline, the easy and quick answer is rarely the correct one. We have to set a good example for our kids, and if we don't want them to bully, humiliate and shame their peers, then we have to avoid those same behaviours ourselves.

"Public shaming is bad parenting—so, stop it!" Emma Waverman, *Today's Parent*, June 7, 2015.

A self-fulfilling prophecy

There is little evidence to demonstrate that the naming of young people will prevent recidivism.

In fact, recent research conducted by Professor Duncan Chappell and myself in the Northern Territory (the only jurisdiction in Australia where juvenile justice provisions permit the naming of youth brought before the courts) presents anecdotal evidence that naming and shaming can have the opposite effect.

In a few instances, young people were actually emboldened in their offending, convinced they had a sullied reputation to live up to.

This view is supported by Russell Goldflam from the Criminal Lawyers Association of the Northern Territory (CLANT) who says there is potential for a "badge of honour" effect from public identification.

For many others though, being named simply brought greater police attention not only to themselves but to their families and communities as well.

Detrimental outcomes for indigenous youth

Professor Chappell and I have noted elsewhere that there are a number of detrimental outcomes arising from any disclosure of juveniles' identities. These include a misuse of the concept of shaming (i.e. stigmatising), the potential for vigilante action, a false sense of community protection, and the possibility of disrupting rehabilitative efforts.

Our research found that youth were rarely named in the media often because of welfare provisions, or because most juvenile offending is petty and lacking in salacious news values. However, some individuals were singled out and, in these instances, there was evidence of repeated naming to the detriment of those young people and their families.

Of particular concern, were Indigenous youth—so grossly over-represented in the juvenile justice system, who were similarly over-represented in those singled out for public identification.

There was evidence too that the naming of these young people meant that sporting scholarships were jeopardised, employment prospects were diminished, and even the capacity for their families to obtain housing was badly affected.

The movement to publicly name juvenile offenders is clearly gathering momentum. We are witnessing the erosion of long-held protections for youthful offenders, and the international conventions that support them. The imperative to rehabilitate and educate young offenders is being ignored, if not abandoned in favour of more politically expedient and popular positions.

> *"There is nothing to be gained in watching another person being hurt. In fact, there's research showing that just observing social cruelty takes a psychological toll."*

Online Shaming Robs People of Their Humanity

Anne Collier

In the following viewpoint, published by the website netfamilynews .org, Anne Collier recommends caution and sensitivity for our online interactions. Since the internet brings together those who ordinarily would not interact, we should use restraint and refrain form snap judgments, since we lack a binding context to moderate such interaction. The article also specifies some basic ground rules for digital etiquette. An example of such as rule is that one should not say something online one would not say in person. The article then enumerates measures to allow children and teens safe participation in online culture. Anne Collier is executive director of the Net Safety Collaborative and founder of iCanHelpline.org. She blogs at NetFamilyNews.org.

As you read, consider the following questions:

1. What does the term "context collapse" mean?
2. What are the rules of social media the article urges us all to heed?
3. Given that bullying is more common "IRL" (in real life), why might more attention be given to online bullying, according to the article?

The public discussion about "online reputation" has gotten darker, as "public shaming" appears in more and more headlines. We may think it's tough to be a celebrity, having everything one does—good, bad or anything in between—go viral. But it's even tougher *not* to be, if you post something negative online. Because when you're not a celebrity, it seems only bad stuff goes viral, not just every little thing you do. A stupid joke, a callous remark, a cranky critical comment gets posted, and the non-celebrity can suddenly find him or herself judged by thousands or (depending on how outrageous the post's seen to be by his/ her new "public") by millions. The public has no context, and so somehow you're *defined*—either intentionally by someone who has it in for you or by a public seeking entertainment on a slow news day—by something bad you mindlessly or angrily said.

Not that this new set of conditions excuses callous or casually cruel remarks made online. But if jobs are lost, depression or self-harm happens, reputations are destroyed and the safety of the commenter and his or her family and friends is threatened—all of which has happened to people—it is at least legitimate to ask if the punishment fits the "crime." That's an important question raised in a book excerpt about public shaming in this week's *New York Times Magazine*. It leads with the story of how a p.r. executive with a Twitter following of just 170 people became a global celebrity while she was on an international flight. That a racist comment, whether reportedly a joke or not, could be posted publicly and by a p.r. professional on the way to South Africa is astonishing, but so was the scale of the collective response.

Our humanity, not our technology

Since what happens in social media is much more about our humanity than our technology, we really need to think together about the punishment humanity is now capable of meting out.

Public humiliation as public spectacle is as old as humanity. A clever Times Magazine editor headlined the article "Feed Frenzy," but it trivializes the fact that public shaming in newsfeeds has a potential reach and distribution speed never before seen by the human race. Even historically, though, being in the crowd was more than a spectacle—more than merely a witnessing—because the crowd, the public part of the shaming, was what created the shame. Now, even as the number of potential witnesses has grown exponentially, so has the ease of participation and harm.

"Harassment as a whole, and the way in which it impacts individuals, fundamentally changes the arc of people's lives. Economically, socially and politically," author and law professor Danielle Citron told writer Soraya Chemaly in a Salon .com interview.

Who's being degraded?

Collectively, we haven't thought enough—much less taught our children—about who's being degraded and harmed. In crowd-sourced media, the crowd, the media and the community are degraded and harmed too.

Because these digital spaces are available to everyone, are shared and social on a global scale, we are all hurt by public shaming. Ultimately and contrary to what some shamers seem to think, there is nothing to be gained in watching another person being hurt. In fact, there's research showing that just observing social cruelty takes a psychological toll.

"Bystanders are significantly affected by the bullying they witness or hear about, so much so that they may be at an increased risk of self-harming behavior," wrote Prof. Ian Rivers at Brunel University in the UK. He and his fellow researchers found higher rates of depression, substance abuse and anxiety among students who had witnessed bullying. "The single most significant predictor of suicide risk among bystanders was found to be *powerlessness*[emphasis his]."

See it for what it is

So the need to address digital public shaming is getting more urgent. People are getting hurt. Second chances are going away. We can't afford to let our children grow up believing online harassment and public humiliation are just the way things are. Knowledge is power, so here are some things to remember:

The old-fashioned word is "ignominy": It was used by a signer of the Declaration of Independence, Benjamin Rush, in a 1787 paper calling for its end, according to the Times Magazine article, but "pillory and whippings weren't abolished at the federal level until 1839." One of its definitions is "public contempt." It takes away people's dignity, marginalizes and dehumanizes people. One of its antidotes is emotional intelligence. "We need to teach [our kids] how to be socially competent in a very complex world," said author Rosalind Wiseman in a talk about raising boys. "Abuse of power is inevitable, so it's our job to teach them social competency, to teach them that people's dignity is not negotiable, for them or for anyone."

There are invisible publics: Social media researcher danah boyd famously wrote about these in her 2008 PhD dissertation—that people and groups you never even thought of can instantly become your "public" or audience online.

Contexts melt into each other online. The academic term is "context collapse," and it was also central to boyd's dissertation. It means your public or interest group or community can quickly mash up with an entirely different one, both finding themselves oddly thrown together in the same context, where they'd never find themselves together offline.

Snap judgment without context can create a lot of trouble out of what you post, when combined with people's ability to instantly repost, retweet, forward, twist and share it with…

Instant mass distribution making it go viral and turning snap judgment into *viral* snap judgment and invisible publics into *massive* invisible publics.

If public shaming happens to you or your child, do not take your appeal to the court of public opinion. A dad did that on YouTube after his daughter was bullied, and then things really went south for him and everybody, the *Minneapolis Star-Tribune* reported. Remember that all the above holds true. Snap judgment, no context, etc., etc. can turn victims into perpetrators in the contextless public mind, and vice versa. Seeking sympathy or retribution in social media can backfire horribly.

Rule No. 1 for empathy in social media

Maybe public forgiveness will eclipse public shaming. But until we get there, we need to be completely clear and to teach our children that those are fellow human beings with feelings and lives behind those tweets, posts, texts, comments and images. That's Rule No. 1.

"Inability to see a face is, in the most direct way, inability to recognize shared humanity with another," according to a Valentine's Day essay in the *New York Times*. [This is why Facebook has been working with "compassion researchers" on how to create empathy in digital spaces where we don't have facial expression to enable it]

Two more basic rules of the road

"A world stripped of faces is a world stripped, not merely of ethics, but of the biological and cultural foundations of ethics," continues Stephen Marche, the Times essay's writer. "We need a new art of conversation for the new conversations we are having."

So Marche offers two simple rules for overcoming facelessness. Besides Rule No. 1 about always seeing human beings behind texts, tweets and posts, these might help us and our children grow resilience and civility, see public shaming for what it is and help reduce its impact: "Never say anything online that you wouldn't say to somebody's face" and "Don't listen to what people wouldn't say to your face." Because it's much more about them than it is about you. So if you don't like it, it's not worth your time or attention.

A few further thoughts for parents & educators

The flipside of that disempowerment is to empower our children (and all social media users) with knowledge, agency and literacy— knowledge of what public shaming is and does, agency for doing something about it (sometimes that's comforting a target publicly or anonymously, sometimes it's counter speech or countering the cruelty) and literacy for taking intelligent action (with media and social-emotional skills).

Avoidance doesn't get our children to that empowerment. Parents may want to be aware that not only does banning social media hamper resilience and skill development, it can increase the risk of social marginalization for children whose social circles are in social media. Better to know what's going on in the peer group and learn how to navigate the digital parts of social life as well as the in-person parts. Just like adults, a child can develop "FOMO" (fear of missing out) with or without social media, but there can be more acute FOMO outside of the social fray. According to researcher Stan Davis, co-author of the Youth Voice Project "isolation and ostracism is the core wound in peer mistreatment."

None of this is to say there's greater risk of social cruelty online than offline. It just has much greater exposure. Ethan Zuckerman at the MIT Media Lab wrote, "The internet creates an environment where we are aware of speech we otherwise wouldn't hear." We have data showing that bullying is no worse online. In fact, it's worse *offline*. The Centers for Disease Control published research last June showing that 19.6% of high school students had experienced bullying on school grounds in the past year vs. 14.8% who'd experienced it online. But the digital versions of harassment and bullying are what we're seeing in the news. So it's just as possible that we're collectively reacting to the greater exposure of negative behaviors as to increased negativity. What that means for parents is a greater than ever need to ask our kids about any negativity they're personally experiencing (and possibly participating in) online and respond to that rather than extrapolate from headlines what their experiences are.

Because your children's and everybody's experiences in social media are very individual—they have everything to do with who they are, who their friends are, how they behave there, and how everybody relates to one another offline as well as online.

> "A spanking, a haircut, or standing
> on a corner announcing one's failures
> will not protect Black children; it only
> gives parents the sense of security
> that is elusive in a racist and violent
> nation."

Shamed Children of Color May Internalize Racist Cultural Standards

Stacey Patton

In the following viewpoint, Stacey Patton provides an insightful look at how and why some African American parents are using shame as a disciplinary tool for their children. In a racist culture, Patton argues that even a punishment as seemingly innocuous as a funny old man haircut can have serious ramifications. Moreover, African American youth are often perceived as more "adult," leaving them vulnerable to threats from police. For these reasons, Patton is alarmed by parents who abnegate their responsibilities to be healthy caregivers and cites a number of reasons why shaming children has lasting negative consequences on a child's emotional well being. Stacey Patton is a writer, author, speaker, and college professor.

"Dear Black People: Please Stop Shaming Your Kids on Social Media," Stacey Patton, The DAME Magazine. Reprinted by permission.

As you read, consider the following questions:

1. Why might some in the African American community applaud parents who shame their children?
2. On the other hand, why might others claim these parents are doing harm to their kids?
3. How does the author tie these shaming episodes to a backdrop of racist culture?

W hy are some Black parents publicly shaming their children on social media in the name of responsible discipline and good parenting? And why do so many people find pleasure in the spectacle of violence by watching and sharing the public humiliation of Black youth?

Most Black parents are not guilty of this, but the fact that we're seeing this on our social media feeds means that there are too many.

On the surface, it might seem relatively harmless: A parent photographs his or her child holding up a sign confessing sins like missing a curfew, skipping school, failing a test, dressing provocatively, acting "too grown," lying, and stealing. Private punishment becomes public humiliation as these images go viral. Folks who see and share it applaud the parent for being strict and doing what they can to keep these wayward Black kids out of gangs, prisons, and morgues.

Recently, an Atlanta barber named Russell Frederick has been giving free "Benjamin Button" haircuts out of his A-1 barber shop to kids, whose parents want to use this kind of humiliation as a way to discipline them. Frederick is participating in a longstanding American tradition of public ridicule and demonization of Black boys and girls.

Frederick's method was recently featured on a TV news segment, in which a trio of anchors—a White woman, a White man, and a Black man—debated whether humiliating a child is an effective tool for discipline. The White woman celebrated the approach. The White man challenged it, saying that humiliating children is not a good alternative to spanking. And the Black man—apparently the only parent in the group—said he found it effective when he did this with his teenage son, adding that he would NOT do this to a daughter.

As Frederick told the Washington Post, "Parents are at a loss. When you go to discipline kids these days, they can't necessarily use physical punishment the way parents did in the past, but they have to do something. If you don't, and your kid ends up doing something crazy, everyone is going to say the problems started at home."

Physical abuse has been eliminated from a parent's arsenal because of (White) liberal policies. People are defending this so-called "novel" approach by arguing that the haircut is a creative and non-violent way to convey to their kid that misbehavior has negative consequences. But the logic of this form of punishment embodies an unwillingness to recognize that there are emotional repercussions, not least of which the mental scars that are hard to heal.

The issue isn't just about disciplinary haircuts—although given the nature of Black hair politics, we should reflect on why the significance of waging war on the scalps of Black children is so damaging—but rather the issue of using public humiliation to get children to obey their parents. When the hair of a child is altered in an effort to make them look ridiculous, their peers will ridicule, humiliate, and denigrate them, and this is a form of emotional abuse. Whether it works to curb some children's behavior is less important than the bigger picture, especially when it comes to Black children in the U.S.

Some of the most popular videos circulating on social media portray parents or other family members spanking kids for acting out well within the range of normal and customary childhood infractions. I am an anti-spanking activist, so I pay special attention to these posts and the commentary they generate, which most of the time cheers on the person for teaching that child a lesson.

And that's an even bigger problem: People's need to broadcast their tough-love parenting all over social media. I imagine it bolsters their sense of insecurity and inadequacy in rearing their children, as they seek applause for projecting their strong values and no-nonsense approach. But it also reflects a response to the way Black parents have long been blamed as absent and inadequate, and for social breakdown of our communities. It's an overcorrection, these public displays of extreme disciplining, a declaration to the world, "Look what we are doing; we are parenting, we are demanding disciplined children, so shut the hell up, America."

But the extreme discipline has the potential to make these children more vulnerable to violence, and amps up their risk for behaviors that will get them in trouble at school and on the streets. Not to mention Black children are being killed because of a long heritage of racialized ideas about Black children's bodies, and character.

What boggles my mind about the whack grown-man haircuts is that these parents who are hauling their kids into Frederick's barber shop seem to have forgotten that 12-year-old Tamir Rice is dead because a trigger-happy cop blinded by those racialized ideas mistook him for a 20-year-old man, and his toy gun for a real weapon.

There are numerous studies telling us that Black children are routinely perceived to be older and therefore treated as such, and more likely to be suspended or expelled from school, disciplined much more harshly, locked up, and even shot by police.

Physically altering a small child's appearance not only invites ridicule and shame, but feeds into dangerous and potentially deadly stereotypes and myths putting young people in a dangerous situation in a society where there is little distinction between Black children and adults, and where Black kids are already adultified in the cultural mind-set, and accelerated toward social and physical death.

"Nothing is to be gained by making a child feel ashamed of his or her appearance," says Lisa Aronson Fontes, Ph.D., a senior lecturer at University Without Walls at the University of Massachusetts, and the author of *Child Abuse and Culture.* "It is difficult enough to grow up with a healthy body image in this culture and especially difficult for African-American children. A child whose appearance is altered in this way may end up being an outcast at school and among peers for weeks if not months or years. We want our children to be happy and have solid relationships. We should not do anything that would make them be pushed away by their peers."

There is nothing easy about parenting a Black child today, in large part because of the dangers that all Black children face, especially from the police. So it's understandable that some parents engage in punitive shaming and social-media broadcasting to send the message that they're laying down the law with their child so hopefully the law won't lay their child down forever.

Black parents have been working overtime to send this message to authorities: "I'm doing this job so the criminal justice system won't." This is something Black folks have been engaging in since the plantation.

If only it were that simple. Because doing so creates a false sense of protection playing on White supremacist narratives that locate anti-Blackness at the feet of Black behavior and pathology. In other words, it works from belief that stop-and-frisk, rates of suspension and expulsion, incarceration or death-by-police is rooted in the undisciplined Black body.

The ballot or the spanking?

Ceaseless agitation or old man's haircut?

A spanking, a haircut, or standing on a corner announcing one's failures will not protect Black children; it only gives parents the sense of security that is elusive in a racist and violent nation. Changing Black behavior will not save us. Whipping and humiliation our children will not set us free.

But if the parents of Black children take on the role of overseers, we don't need plantations or the KKK. And when we do something like alter our children's appearance we are participating in a dehumanization process required by a White supremacist society. Public shaming tells our children that they have no right to bodily integrity. It shows our children that they cannot count on their caregivers to protect them. So how then can we expect the larger society to protect our kids?

"My initial reaction is that this public shaming, via social media, and picked up by both mainstream print and broadcast news outlets, is a form of psychological maltreatment," says Nadine Bean, a professor of social work at West Chester University. The videos "are a way to gain temporary fame and kudos. But the impact of psychological maltreatment is well-documented … and lifelong. They can take the form of insults, threats, public shaming, belittling, being emotionally neglectful, being insensitive, cruel, etc."

Those photos and videos on social media might be revealing much more about the parents than their child's disobedient behavior. "A caretaker who posts a video showing him or herself humiliating a child is gloating over holding power over that child," says Aronson Fontes. "This sounds to me like an adult who feels powerless."

While some Black parents might see altering a child's body as a way of protecting them from dangerous behaviors, it's a denial of the child's physical, emotional, identity, and cultural integrity. Given the ways that Black hair is regulated and policed in our society, from Hollywood and the military to the Olympics and corporate boardrooms, we have to be aware of the ramifications of turning hair into an arena of discipline for children who have to navigate a society where all the odds are stacked against their entire selves, including the hair that grows on their heads.

In a moment where we're seeing more news stories about teachers cutting Black children's hair in class, or being suspended for wearing natural hairstyles, do these actions and videos simply extend the reaction of White supremacist efforts to discipline Black youth into the realm of spectacle?

The long-term consequences of this kind of discipline are more serious than most people imagine. Experts analyzing data from the National Child Traumatic Stress Network for the American Psychological Association found that children who experienced psychological maltreatment or emotional abuse, defined as "caregiver-inflicted bullying, terrorizing, coercive control, severe insults, debasement, threats, overwhelming demands, shunning and/or isolation" suffer in their lifetime from heightened levels of depression, anxiety, attachment problems, substance abuse, and low self-esteem.

Shaming and humiliation masquerading as discipline can harm a child's attachment to their parents. According to the National Child Traumatic Stress Network, "Our ability to develop healthy, supportive relationships with friends and significant others depends on our having first developed those kinds of relationships in our families. Through relationships with important attachment figures, children learn to trust others, regulate their emotions, and interact with the world; they develop a sense of the world as safe or unsafe, and come to understand their own value as individuals. When those relationships are unstable or unpredictable, children learn that they cannot rely on others to help them."

There are too many spaces that are already unsafe for Black children. Walking to the store is not safe; getting in a snowball fight is not safe. Being at school and the workplace are not safe; hanging out with friends is not about the innocence afforded to White youth. A home that is not safe and empowering does not change the culture of terror but instead normalizes the violence.

The consequences are not long-term but immediate as well. Trauma experts say that children who do not have healthy attachments have been shown to be more vulnerable to stress. They have trouble controlling and expressing emotions, and may react violently or inappropriately to situations. A child with a complex trauma history may have problems in romantic relationships, in friendships, and with authority figures, such as teachers or police officers.

Ironically, this suggests that Black parents who use these disciplinary tactics might inadvertently be making their children more likely to have problems with the very authority figures they're trying to protect their kids from.

"It is better not to beat children, especially if we don't want them to fight with others," says Aronson Fontes. "Nothing is to be gained by inflicting emotional abuse instead of physical abuse. Instead, we should be using positive discipline."

"There are so many healthier alternatives and none of them involve exploitive images of minor children on social media or mainstream media," says Bean. "Taking away privileges, time outs (one minute per child's age), having the child write (if able) about why his/her choice of behavior was not good and what alternative behaviors might be used in the future, and, of course modeling compassionate, humanistic behaviors even in the throes of conflict. There are always alternatives to harsh physical punishment or psychological maltreatment. ALWAYS!"

There is no upside to shaming and humiliating children in the name of trying to improve their behavior. All children need for their parents, teachers and other caregivers to provide discipline from time to time—that's inevitable.

But with Black children all over the country saying that their greatest wish is "to grow up," and not be murdered by the police; with a generation of Black children coming of age against a backdrop of #BlackLivesMatter and #ICan'tBreathe, we cannot afford to cause our children any kind of harm, especially in the name of good, responsible parenting and protection from a society set on their destruction. #BlackHappinessMatters #BlackSelfEsteemMatters #BlackEmotionalHealthMatters

So while it might seem that giving a child a punitive haircut to change their behavior is a benign alternative to corporal punishment, and a sign of good, responsible parenting, we must look deeper and do better.

Black children are living in a state of siege, and they need their parents and caregivers to be allies, not adversaries, as they struggle to navigate the difficult maze to safe, healthy adulthood in this country. Their lives are at stake merely by virtue of their race, and their futures are perilous. When we begin to spend as much time focusing on what is inside their heads as on top of them; when we invest in their emotional and psychological well-being as if their lives depend on us doing so, then we will begin to move in the right direction.

| "The public shaming that happens to students in our schools has to stop. The reliance on public displays of punishment as a way to control behavior has to stop."

Shame Is Not an Appropriate Tool for the Classroom

Pernille Ripp

In the following viewpoint, a teacher named Pernille Ripp discusses some of her professional and pedagogical strategies on her blog. One method Ripp entirely discredits is classroom shaming. Tactics such as writing student's names on the board when they misbehave and other similar indicators violate what should be a private conversation between teacher and student, according to Ripp. She notes that observing her own child's behavior patterns opened her mind to this insight and urges all teachers to follow her lead. Pernille Ripp is a teacher and blogger.

"On Public Shaming and Our Classrooms," Pernille Ripp, September 24, 2015. Reprinted by permission.

As you read, consider the following questions:

1. What caused the author to reconsider her position on shaming in the classroom?
2. What does the author suggest teachers do instead of shaming students?
3. Does the author provide specifics suggesting this is effective?

I used to yell students' names across the classroom, making sure that everyone knew who was now in trouble. I had the teacher voice down coupled with the stern glance.

I used to have students write their names on the board when they messed up. That name served as a public reminder of their poor decisions all day and showed them that I meant business. It was a wonderful display of who could not figure out how to behave well.

I used to have students call their parents in the middle of class to tell them when they were having a bad day. Three strikes you are out was the way we worked. I figured it didn't matter that the rest of the class could hear their call, after all, that would probably just act as a deterrent for the rest of them.

I did not think I was shaming children, after all, children thrive on rules and routines. Therefore, these rules were definitely helping them become better citizens of our school.

After a year, the names on the board did not seem to work so well, so I switched to sticks in a cup. Everyone started in the green cup, your poor decisions moved you to yellow or red. The sticks never moved backwards and we reset at the end of the day. The names were no longer on the board, but the stick moving, that happened in front of the class. That walk of shame where all eyes were on a child as they were told to "Move their stick" was a daily occurrence. In our classroom everyone knew who the "bad kids" were, and so did their parents, after all, students love to share stories about how so and so got in trouble that day.

Then my firstborn got a little older. She got a little more energy. She wasn't that good at sitting still or even paying attention at times. She had so much to do and so many things to see. And in her, I quickly saw the future. If she got a teacher that used these systems of public shaming, she would be the kid that would move her stick. She would be the kid whose name would be on the board. And I would be that parent, wondering why my child was being publicly shamed for behaviors she was trying so hard to control. For things that she did not do to intentionally harm the instruction, but simply needed support to work through.

So I stopped. I threw it all out. It turns out that you can have classrooms that thrive without the shaming from public punishment. That you can have well-functioning classrooms without the public behavior charts. That students will try to correct behavior and set goals with you when you remove the element of shame and try to problem solve instead. That they will see you as an ally, rather than just a punisher, and that will get you much further when you try to help them become better human beings.

There are only a few things I am willing to fall on the sword for on this blog. Previous experiences have shown me that most ideas in education are not black and white. There are always more than 2 sides to every story, and every teacher teaches differently, and that does not mean they are not good teachers, it just means they are different. But today, I will make an exception.

The public shaming that happens to students in our schools has to stop. The reliance on public displays of punishement as a way to control behavior has to stop. And the first place we stop it is by getting rid of public behavior charts. Those clip systems that tell the whole world something that should be a private conversation between a teacher, a student, and the parents.

Whether it is a clip-system, the move-your-stick, the flip-your-card, or the put-your-name-on-the-board, and yes I used most of them myself, we have to find a better way. We have to try because we are creating schools where children hate coming. Where parents worry that their child will be singled out for having energy, for being excited, for not being able to sit still all day. Where teachers are forced into roles as enforcers rather than nurturers. I know that there needs to be consequences. I know that we have to help students navigate behavior in our classrooms, but there are better ways then asking a child to create a permanent reminder and public display of how they are having a very bad day.

I am not proud of the mistakes I have made as a teacher. I am not proud of the things I have tried that have hurt children rather than helped them. But I am willing to write about it in the hopes that it will start a dialogue. That perhaps someone, somewhere, will take a moment to rethink something that seems to be so ingrained in our classrooms. That perhaps this post will help someone wonder what they can do instead. Because there is so much that can be done instead, there are so many ways to build community, to build better relationships, to still have consequences, and create classrooms where kids have a chance at thriving. All kids, not just the ones that know how to behave. But we have to take the first step. We have to take down the charts, remove the cups, erase the names. We have to create classrooms that do not run on shame, but run on community. I speak not just from my teacher heart, but from that of a parent. Our children deserve better than this. And it starts with us. Even if it makes us nervous. Even if we are not sure of what to do instead. I will help. Just ask.

| *"Discipline is not only constant but also public."*

Kids Want Discipline, Not Shame

Jennifer Keys Adair

In the following viewpoint, Jennifer Keys Adair argues that public shaming and other dramatic punishment techniques are not effective methods for teachers. Strict rules and discipline are enforced for a variety of reasons, but ironically they get in the way of learning. Dialogue and participation, not simply obedience, are the keys to learning. Jennifer Keys Adair, Ph.D., is an assistant professor of early childhood education at the University of Texas at Austin, a young scholar fellow with the Foundation for Child Development, and a public voices fellow with the OpEd Project.

As you read, consider the following questions:

1. What do kids believe about discipline, according to the State of Kids survey?
2. What examples of public discipline does the author give?
3. What are the differences in discipline for white children and children of color?

"Why Disciplining Kids Can Be So Tricky for Parents and Teachers," Jennifer Keys Adair, *The Conversation*, October 14, 2015. https://theconversation.com/why-disciplining -kids-can-be-so-tricky-for-parents-and-teachers-49083. Licensed under CC BY ND 4.0 International.

D isciplining works if it is not over the top and children understand the point of it.

Highlights magazine's annual State of Kids survey found that a majority of children appreciated being disciplined and believed that it helped them behave better.

What children disagreed with were the strategies that were used by their parents—the most common ones being time-outs and taking away electronics. The report suggests that disciplining strategies work better when they open up communication and strengthen relationships among friends or siblings or between kids and adults.

However, my own work as an education professor and researcher who works with schools and families shows that disciplining is becoming a major issue at schools too, taking up more and more of the school day. So, why are schools imposing severe disciplinary measures?

What's going on in schools?

Let's first look at what disciplining looks like in schools.

Many schools now have lines on the floor that students must walk on to get anywhere. Some schools even have tape on the ground to show where students should walk in the classroom. Hallways have stop signs at each corner and schools enforce zero noise zones.

Children are told to hold air in cheeks like a bubble when walking in the hallways or when they are supposed to be listening to instructions or storytime. They are told to walk straight, not touch anyone, keep their hands to themselves, sit on an X mark on the floor, raise a hand before speaking, keep eyes on the teacher, use only one piece of paper, follow directions and be quiet.

Over the past 10 years, strange discipline measures such as red, yellow and green lights, where green means well-done and red means bad behavior, have become commonplace. Children can get their recess taken away or be put into an isolation room. Or, increasingly, even the police can be called.

Discipline is not only constant but also public. Just last week, I was in a class where a child's name was on the board. Children at my table pointed it out to me and explained that the kid gets in trouble a lot. They told me that the teacher writes his name on the board and then when he is good, he gets one letter erased. When they are all erased, he can have free time.

So why are there such heavy amounts of discipline at school?

The unfortunate fact is that there is an extraordinary amount of content that teachers are supposed to cover during a school year. Usually, school districts give teachers eight-week plans that tell them what to cover and when.

This means that children, whether they like it or not, need to learn with the speed, level and topic choices determined by adults who don't know them. Children have to sit still and focus for extraordinary lengths of time.

Given the pressure on teachers, discipline becomes a larger and larger part of the school day, just to get kids to get through what is required by the state or Common Core guidelines.

So, instead of encouraging children to engage with content, lessons or materials, teachers find themselves having to discipline them into it.

Perhaps the most troubling part of discipline at schools is how unfairly it is given out.

Who gets the most disciplined?

This emphasis on obedience over learning is more likely to be found in classrooms with a majority of children from marginalized communities.

Not only is heavy discipline starting younger and younger, it is also worse for children of color.

In fact, suspensions now begin in prekindergarten. And almost 50% of those suspended are African-American kids.

As educational psychologist Kevin Cokley has pointed out, "There is a conspiracy against black children in our schools." Curiously, girls of color are suspended six times more often than

THE LONG-LASTING EFFECTS OF SHAME

Parents are tapping into that fear of embarrassment with a new form of punishment: public humiliation. In the age of social media, it's remarkably easy to punish children on a platform that exposes them to their peers, other adults and even strangers.

While public humiliation may be effective, there are other ways to punish children without turning them into a spectacle.

Public humiliation is scarring, especially in cases when images go viral. It may stop children from repeating bad behavior, but the shame also plagues them long after they've learned their lesson and the family has moved on from the incident. To other adults and children who've witnessed the punishment, the offending child becomes that "kid who took a photo with his father's bottle" or "the girl who snuck out at 3AM." That label could stick for years, especially in small towns.

It's also callous. What if adult transgressions—infidelity, poor money management, drug abuse to name a few—were plastered for everyone to see? Imagine the degradation and shame that we would feel, and how much harder it would be to better ourselves with the world watching and judging. That's the kind of ordeal that publicly humiliated children go through at the most impressionable time in their lives. I'm sure the kids who were ridiculed in front of thousands of strangers would take a spanking over shame any day.

"Shame and Social Media: Should Parents Use Public Humiliation as Discipline?" Jessica C. Andrews, Clutch, December 7, 2012.

white girls. They are even disciplined more than white boys starting in the early grades.

This is not because children of color, in particular African-American children, are somehow more disobedient or rebellious than white children. It is because often, even when teachers don't mean to, children's behavior is interpreted differently.

White teachers notice black children first and often adopt society's portrayals of communities of color as problematic or out of control. Over 80% of teachers are white in public schools.

And there is little preparation for teachers to be positive, culturally engaged and anti-racist in classrooms.

How discipline gets in the way of learning

If most of what children hear are teachers trying to get everyone to sit still, be quiet and listen to directions, what does this teach them about learning and being a learner?

In my work on how young children use their agency (the ability to make decisions at school), I find that most children describe learning as following directions. As one child explained, "Learning is quiet."

Children often see obedience as the point of school. In fact, teachers and students both tell me that they can tell children are learning when their "eyes are on the teacher."

Of course, just because a child is obedient doesn't mean they are learning.

If a classroom has a ton of rules and a narrow range of acceptable behavior (kids cannot get materials for themselves, help out classmates without permission, etc) then there are only a few behaviors that will not get someone in trouble. In such a scenario, there is much more likelihood for disobedience and more discipline.

The creation of such narrow spaces make it difficult for children to show a variety of skills, demonstrate capabilities or use a variety of coping skills when they are frustrated.

Just as the State of Kids survey pointed out, conversation is critical to discipline. Some schools are trading suspensions for dialogue. And it has resulted in much success. Instead of jumping to discipline, these administrators and teachers are encouraging their students to problem solve and participate in making the situation better as part of the school community.

What parents, teachers can do

Classrooms need to be spaces where children can participate in fixing issues and taking initiative. Children need not be punished and taken away from the classroom.

Similar lessons can be applied at home. Parents can stress on discipline that focuses on hard work and not taking a break. Engaging kids through conversations, projects and helping out will emphasize learning more than discipline.

And the results will be well worth it.

Periodical and Internet Sources Bibliography

The following articles have been selected to supplement the diverse views presented in this chapter.

Ariadne Brill, "Shame Does Not Teach Children to Do Better," Positive Parenting Connection, May 21, 2013. http://www .positiveparentingconnection.net/shame-does-not-teach -children-to-do-better.

Robin Grille and Beth Macgregor, "'Good' Children—At What Price? The Secret Cost of Shame," The Natural Child Project, Retrieved September 2016. http://www.naturalchild.org/robin_grille/good_ children.html.

Robert King, "Is Public Shaming of Your Child Effective? Right?" IndyStar, August 23, 2015. http://www.indystar.com/story/ news/2015/08/23/public-shaming-child-effective -right/32148623.

Bedford E. F. Palmer II, Ph.D., "Good Parenting Does Not Involve Public Shaming," DrBFPalmer.com. http://www.drbfpalmer .com/blog/good-parenting-does-not-involve-public-shaming -an-authoritative-alternative-to-emotional-abuse.

Jameson Parker, "13-Year-Old Girl Commits Suicide After Dad Posts Public Shaming Video Online," Addicting Info.org, June 4, 2015. http://addictinginfo.org/2015/06/04/13-year-old-girl-commits -suicide-after-dad-posts-public-shaming-video-online-video.

S. E. Smith, "Parents, Stop Publicly Shaming Your Kids on the Internet," The Daily Dot, June 5, 2015. http://www.dailydot.com/ opinion/isabel-laxamana-suicide-shaming-video.

CHAPTER 3

Should the Media Engage in Public Shaming?

Chapter Preface

Social media sites such as Facebook and Twitter allow individuals to expose and shame bad behavior with relative ease and anonymity. Unfortunately, once a social media "call-out" has been made, it cannot be taken back. When an instance of internet shaming spirals out of control, those who may see themselves as societal underdogs fighting for justice find the script flipped. Now, ironically, it is they who are leading the angry mob. And while it may be difficult to muster sympathy for those who have displayed racist or sexist behavior, when retributive shaming reaches a fever pitch, no one wins. In fact, all too often, lives are permanently ruined.

The stories may be familiar by now: a woman posts a photo of two men making sexist comments at a conference and all lose their jobs; teens make racist comments about President Obama and the remarks follow them forever; a woman traveling to South Africa makes a distasteful joke about AIDS and finds herself unemployed and estranged from her friends and family upon arrival. Do these episodes constitute justice in the digital age, or something out of proportion to the original offense?

One way to evaluate this question is by taking into account the position of the offender. Is this person a political pundit, influential media personality, celebrity, or other public figure with a large audience? Or is it a young person trying however misguidedly to impress or provoke a limited audience? In the former case, shaming is arguably appropriate. Media personalities influence what people think and how they behave. Obviously, the threat of being shamed and losing a platform is a powerful deterrent from behaving in ways we agree are unacceptable. However, for those inclined to espouse hateful views, a shaming from those they perceive as opponents may only embolden them. In some cases, shame has no sway. Indeed, as the rise of Donald Trump in the

2016 presidential campaign demonstrated, the more outlandish the statement, the more attention it will draw, feeding a perverse cycle.

In practice, few have the luxury of leveraging shame for personal gain. Most who are shamed have little recourse to expensive PR firms or other means of online reputation rehabilitation available to celebrities. A shaming incident can therefore haunt a person indefinitely, making the basics of life such as finding a job nearly impossible, as noted in some testimonials that follow.

For this reason, when we discuss public shaming in the media, it is important to mind a distinction between traditional media, in which people have a comparatively powerful loudspeaker, and social media, where ordinary people can find their lives ruined. Given the vast and unpredictable nature of the internet, most experts urge caution before calling out inappropriate behavior. Nonetheless, we still should discourage hateful and offensive speech, acts, and behavior. The articles that follow all address this question in some way but reach subtle conclusions.

| "Online shaming is a door that swings only one way: You may have the power to open it, but you don't have the power to close it."

Online Shaming Is a Kind of Bullying

Laura Hudson

In the following viewpoint, Laura Hudson cautions against online shaming by the media. Even if the original act is reprehensible, the author claims that online shaming amplifies the original "call-out" to an unfair degree. She uses the now infamous case of the PyCon tech conference as an example: a woman with several thousand Twitter followers posted an example of crude and possibly sexist behavior. Within a short time, all involved lost their jobs. The author is not excusing bad behavior but admonishing those who call out such behavior to be mindful of their own power, lest they replicate the same bullying they would otherwise condemn. Laura Hudson is a regular contributor to Wired, Slate, *and others.*

"Why You Should Think Twice Before Shaming Anyone on Social Media," Laura Hudson, *Wired,* July 24, 2013. Reprinted by permission.

As you read, consider the following questions:

1. Why does the author argue that social media shaming is often a disproportionate retaliation for the original offense?

2. How does social media act as a "megaphone" amplifying the scope of communication?

3. Is internet shaming always bullying? Are there any conditions under which shaming might be appropriate? If so, what might these be, according to the author?

E arlier this year, at a tech conference called PyCon, the consultant Adria Richards overheard some indelicate puns—involving the terms "dongles" and "forking"—from a couple of male attendees sitting behind her. The jokes made Richards uncomfortable, so in the heat of the moment she decided to register her displeasure by tweeting a picture of the two guys, calling their behavior "not cool."

In the context of a tech culture that often fails to make women feel welcome, it's easy to see why Richards, sitting there in the (roughly 80 percent male) PyCon audience, felt like she wasn't the one with the power in that room.

But online it was a different story. The two men were social-media nobodies, whereas Richards had more than 9,000 Twitter followers, some highly connected in the tech world. Her grievance quickly received more than 100 retweets and press coverage that stretched from The Washington Post to MSNBC.

PyCon soon responded—sympathetically—to her complaint, but the damage was done. One of the men was recognized by his employer and lost his job. The backlash against his firing then triggered a massive onslaught of online abuse against Richards, who also got fired. No one emerged happy. "I have three kids, and I really liked that job," wrote the newly unemployed jokester. "Let this serve as a message to everyone, our actions and words, big or small, can have a serious impact." Later, Richards made a similar assessment: "I don't think anyone who was part of what happened at PyCon that day could possibly have imagined how this issue would have exploded into the public consciousness ... I certainly did not, and now ... the severest of consequences have manifested."

Shaming, it seems, has become a core competency of the Internet, and it's one that can destroy both lives and livelihoods. But the question of who's responsible for the destruction—the person engaging in the behavior or the person revealing it—depends on whom you ask. At its best, social media has given a voice to the disenfranchised, allowing them to bypass the gatekeepers of power and publicize injustices that might otherwise remain invisible. At its worst, it's a weapon of mass reputation destruction, capable of amplifying slander, bullying, and casual idiocy on a scale never before possible.

The fundamental problem is that many shamers, like Richards, don't fully grasp the power of the medium. It's a problem that lots of us need to reckon with: There are millions of Twitter accounts with more than 1,000 followers, and millions on Facebook with more than 500 friends. The owners of those accounts might think they're just regular people, whispering to a small social circle. But in fact they're talking through megaphones that can easily be turned up to a volume the entire world can hear.

Increasingly, our failure to grasp our online power has become a liability—personally, professionally, and morally. We need to think twice before we unleash it.

When Does Shaming Become Bullying?

Consider a form of shaming that a lot of us might want to get behind: calling out people who say indefensibly terrible things online. Numerous Tumblr and Twitter accounts have cropped up to document racist and sexist remarks on social media. Following a feed like @EverydaySexism or @YesYoureRacist can be a powerful experience; after a while, the shocking ugliness fades to a dull, steady ache, an emotional corrosion that simulates how the dehumanization of prejudice can become almost mundane. These feeds shame the jerks they highlight by broadcasting their ignorance far beyond their typically small, like-minded audiences to tens of thousands of people.

When the website Jezebel cataloged a series of racist tweets by high school students about President Obama, it not only published their names but also called their high schools and notified the principals about their tweets. In some cases, Jezebel listed the hobbies and activities of the students, essentially "SEO-shaming" them to potential colleges. Most of the kids have since deleted their Twitter accounts, but search any of their names on Google and you'll likely find references to their racist tweets within the first few results.

Yes, what these kids wrote was reprehensible. But does a 16-year-old making crude comments to his friends deserve to be pilloried with a doggedness we typically reserve for politicians and public figures—or, at the very least, for adults?

We despise racism and sexism because they bully the less powerful, but at what point do the shamers become the bullies? After all, the hallmark of bullying isn't just being mean. It also involves a power differential: The bully is the one who's punching down.

And this is precisely the differential that so many of us fail to grasp when our friends and followers are just abstract numbers on a social-media profile. Indeed, the online elite don't always wield the same sort of social power and influence in their offline lives and jobs; many have been victims of bullying themselves.

When Mike "Gabe" Krahulik, the artist behind the popular webcomic *Penny Arcade,* heard that an unprofessional PR rep for a game controller had been insulting and taunting one of his readers, he gleefully posted the damning emails to his website, along with the man's Twitter name, for the express purpose of unleashing the Internet kraken.

"I have a real problem with bullies," Krahulik wrote, after the marketer was deluged with hate mail. "I spent my childhood moving from school to school and I got made fun of every place I landed. I feel like he is a bully and maybe that's why I have no sympathy here. Someday every bully meets an even bigger bully, and maybe that's me in this case."

But even if you think your bullying is serving a greater good, the fact remains that you're still just a bully.

The Bully Is the One Punching Down.

Internet speech can be cruder and crueler than our real-life interactions, in large part due to our literal distance from the people we're talking to and their reactions. That detachment can sometimes be liberating, and it's often a good thing that people speak bluntly online, especially against injustice that they see around them. But a sense of proportion is crucial. These days, too many Internet shame campaigns dole out punishment that is too brutal for the crime. Using an influential social media account to call out individuals, as Richards did, isn't simply saying something is "not cool"; it's a request to have someone put in the digital stocks, where a potentially unlimited number of people can throw digital stones at them. And it turns out to have real-life consequences for everyone involved.

That's why starting a shaming campaign is not a decision to be taken lightly—especially because the Internet doesn't do take-backs if you change your mind later. The bigger the so-called Donglegate story became, the more disproportionate and unfair Richards' original tweet seemed, even if that level of exposure was never her intent. As Krahulik wrote after the PR bully pleaded with him to make the abuse stop, "Once I had posted the emails I didn't have the power anymore. The Internet had it now, and nothing I said or did was going to change that."

Online shaming is a door that swings only one way: You may have the power to open it, but you don't have the power to close it. And sometimes what rushes through that door can engulf you too.

> *"The 'mob' is making a resurgence, but where they once hurled stones, they now use new media tools to inflict indelible marks of humiliation."*

Public Shaming Is an Abuse of the Media's Power

Kristy Hess and Lisa Waller

In the following viewpoint, Kristy Hess and Lisa Waller use Australian media personality Derryn Hinch as a starting point for a discussion on public shaming by members of the media. The increasing practice of public shaming is bad enough, they argue, when performed by ordinary citizens given a voice on social media. But when those who enjoy a broader platform, such as media professionals and celebrities, use their power to publicly shame others, the inequities—and the consequences—are greater. Kristy Hess and Lisa Waller are senior lecturers in journalism at Deakin University in Australia. Their research on media and journalism has been published in Australia and internationally.

As you read, consider the following questions:

1. What did the soccer fan do to spark the incidents mentioned in the article?
2. Aside from being fined, what was the fan's less conventional punishment?
3. Why do the authors use historical examples of shaming when discussing the media's power to shame?

Australia's "human headline" Derryn Hinch built his fame in radio and television by—often controversially—"naming and shaming" those he subjected to the media blowtorch.

But today, Hinch, as do many others, prefer to use social media tools to publicly humiliate people for behaviour they find unacceptable. There are recent examples of people filming racist behaviour on public transport. There's even footage of people urinating in public places. Citizens upload their shame files into digital space and traditional media lap up the content.

Take the case of Brisbane NRL fan Kerry Ann Strasser. After a few drinks at a State of Origin game in 2011, Strasser pulled down her pants and urinated on her seat. A spectator captured the act on his phone camera and uploaded the footage to YouTube.

The video went viral within hours, scoring 30,000 hits, but was removed a day later as part of the site's policy on inappropriate content. But just as the footage disappeared from YouTube, traditional media intensified her shame by reporting the incident across Australia and the globe. And while her face is not recognisable on the YouTube clip, Strasser was named in mainstream media coverage.

Melbourne radio station 3AW took the lead, reloading the content back onto YouTube and to its own website. Its report included a short piece to air from journalist Seb Costello, who said:

> I'm all for sitting on the edge of your seat at the footy, but surely this is taking the piss!

The Brisbane Magistrates Court heard Suncorp Stadium was alerted to the YouTube footage and provided police with CCTV evidence used to identify her seat. Strasser admitted to being the person in the clip, but instead of issuing an on-the-spot fine, police summonsed her to court on one count of urinating in a public place.

Strasser did not attend, but a number of journalists did. Her lawyer, who entered a plea of guilty on her behalf, told magistrate Wally Ehrich of her client's humiliation and suffering. She said Strasser's family had also been affected "with anyone who knows her being aware she was the woman in the clip." The magistrate acknowledged her "worldwide embarrassment" and fined her A$100 without conviction.

But Strasser's walk of shame continues. Type her name into Google today, and the top results continue to reveal details of her antisocial behaviour. There are also links to web pages that describe her as a "feral bogan."

Our research examines the intensified role of the media in shaming ordinary people when they commit minor crimes. Unlike some North American jurisdictions, Australian courts do not consider public shaming when sentencing. It is the news media that decides if a person who appears before the court will also be brought to wider public attention and the degree to which they will be shamed.

Our research is also particularly concerned with the role of the media in reporting non-convictions. When someone like Strasser receives a non-conviction it means they are given a "second chance" at keeping their criminal record clean. For example, they are not required to reveal their misdemeanour when applying for a job.

However, they can still have an indefinite "media record" imposed on them. We have uncovered numerous examples of people who received non-convictions for minor offences, like stealing a tea towel from Kmart or jaywalking. But they still had their names plastered across Google by traditional and social media outlets. We question whether the unfettered power to impose this punishment fits the nature of the crime.

In western societies, shaming has always been a popular and arguably effective means of social control. Up until the 19th century, shaming penalties were popular punishments for minor crimes. It was a common custom to put offenders in the stocks at a public market and it was not unusual for an angry crowd to pelt them to death.

When these brutal punishments were eventually phased out, the practice of shaming became the domain of the news media—and it's been that way in Australia ever since. However, the practice of shaming is changing again. The "mob" is making a resurgence, but where they once hurled stones, they now use new media tools to inflict indelible marks of humiliation.

Traditional news outlets step in and use their power to further "name and shame." Cases such as Strasser and others that we have encountered provide rich examples of how the fusion of new and old media intensifies the pillorying effect on ordinary people who commit minor crimes.

The old saying that "today's newspaper is tomorrow's fish 'n' chip wrapper" no longer applies. Content is archived across digital spaces from news websites to Google and internet blogs, which means for people like Strasser that their shame is only ever a mouse click away.

> "At face value, this idea that calling out these racists will teach them a lesson seems legit, until you think about the real effects of this kind of social media shaming."

Online Shaming Is Becoming Too Widespread

Fruzsina Eordogh

In the following viewpoint within a by-now familiar debate, Fruzsina Eordogh questions whether trending Tumblr blogs such as Hello There, Racists! are accomplishing anything positive. On the one hand, those who violate social conventions may deserve to be singled out for their bad behavior. However, Eordogh wonders whether in our polarized landscape, this practice may simply embolden those predisposed to insensitive behavior. Moreover, as our culture leans harder on shaming, will the scope of those shamed grow in amount and degree? If we end up shaming people for minor transgressions, this may not be as progressive of a development as it may seem. Fruzsina Eordogh is a freelance digital culture and technology journalist covering various internet phenomena.

"Shaming Racists on Social Media Continues with New Tumblr," Fruzsina Eordogh, Readwrite, November 15, 2012.

As you read, consider the following questions:

1. What is a "doxxing," and which sites discussed in the article take part in this practice?
2. Why do some people argue that those shamed online will just become emboldened?
3. How does the author characterize the shift in online shaming over the past few years?

Hello There, Racists! is the hot new Tumblr everyone is talking about on Twitter. Best New Tumblr, they are calling it. Like much of the digital vigilantism happening since President Obama's re-election, this particular trending Tumblr is about shaming racists.

What It Is

Hello There, Racists! began on November 11, but didn't seem to pick up steam until Wednesday, after it was tweeted by Jeremy Botter, the editor of the Houston Chronicle's Brawl sports blog, quickly followed by K. Thor Jensen, the award-winning writer, illustrator, and influential Twitter user. The Tumblr has, at press time, shamed 60 people based on their racist tweets. The blog collects not just the alleged racists offensive online remarks, but all publicly available information about them. This includes pictures from their Facebook page, as well as where they live and what high school they go to. (A solid majority of the people being shamed are high schoolers.)

The About page for Hello There, Racists! claims that because the "(un)official motto of the GOP is 'personal responsibility,'" these racists "words, names and faces" will "be documented so that they may be responsible for them." Tweets about the Tumblr show people are even writing letters to school officials to let them know their students are behaving in a racist manner online. To those familiar with Internet lingo, this here is a "doxxing."

The Undoing of Pax Dickinson

Business Insider Chief Technology Officer Pax Dickinson ... had a long history of outrageous Twitter comments that were a mix of deliberate provocation and controversial opinions. His precipitous downfall began when those tweets caught the attention of a writer for Valleywag/Gawker, who described Dickinson as "your new tech bro nightmare."

[...]

To this day, he remains essentially unemployable. He says he has received about a dozen enthusiastic job offers that quickly fizzled after he informed his would-be employers of his 15 minutes of infamy. He has worked on several freelance projects that he cannot put on his resume because the companies that hired him don't want it known that he worked for them. He and his wife, Kelly, currently depend primarily on her small income from a home-based business selling fine china.

"Is it fair that Business Insider fired me? Sure," says Dickinson. "I made the company look bad. Having those libertarian sympathies, I don't think anyone should have to employ someone they don't want to employ. But I think being blacklisted and pressure being put on any company that might consider hiring me is a much different issue."

Some influential figures who champion progressive causes in the tech industry have openly encouraged the blacklisting. Shortly after Dickinson's downfall, technologist and blogger Anil Dash wrote, "If you're a venture capitalist, and you invest in Pax's startup without a profound, meaningful and years-long demonstration of responsibility from Pax beforehand, you're complicit in extending the tech industry's awful track record of exclusion, and it's unacceptable."

Shevinsky strongly disagrees. "I worry about efforts to ostracize people from the community," she wrote to me. "What does it mean if we try to take the right to work away from people with opinions that we find dangerous?"

"The Social Media Shaming of Pax Dickinson," Cathy Young, RealClearPolitics, July 8, 2015.

Is This A Good Thing?

While it might make Web citizens feel good to tell off some jerks on the Internet, is online naming and harassment really the way to go? Matt Buchanan thinks so, and said as much in his Buzzfeed piece titled "Why Social Media Shaming Is Okay," written in response to a Twitter debate over my musings prompted by the second annual International Digital Ethics Symposium.

Buchanan writes social media shaming is OK because "the consensus is rapidly crystallizing that the rules and sensibilities of the rest of our lives should largely apply online as well." (Ironically, Buchanan doesn't think the rules and sensibilities journalists practice in real life regarding minors should apply to online coverage.) At face value, this idea that calling out these racists will teach them a lesson seems legit, until you think about the real effects of this kind of social media shaming.

Feeding A Persecution Complex

"A feeling of persecution does wonders to embolden someone," said Jon Hendren, a well-known Internet troll, constant retweeter of teen bad behavior, and writer for the Web culture forum Something Awful. (Hendren distinguishes himself from the vigilante Tumblr by saying what he does is an "exhibition and not 'Hey, lets find these [jerks] and publish where they live'" and added he repeatedly asks his followers to not engage with the people he retweets.)

"I mean, put yourself in the racist jerk's shoes for a second," wrote Hendren in gchat. "You post something terrible, and a bunch of progressive/liberal/whatever folks come out of the woodwork to mess with you. You'd be like 'Well I must be on the right track if these people I didn't like in the first place hate me.'"

Why Bother?

So why are we even bothering to shame someone on social media anyway? Two years ago harassing someone online for something they did, when 4chan and Anonymous did it, was frowned upon by many media outlets. In my impromptu gchat with Hendren, I asked him why he thinks vigilantism is now not only mainstream, but suddenly cool to do.

"Ironically, I think it has to do with the portrayal of 'cyberbullies' in the last few years," wrote Hendren. "It's become okay to go after people being mean on the Internet in the eyes of the law in some places, so why not go after people saying other horrible things?"

Media outlets have been unmasking trolls for more than a year now, the most recent and infamous being Violentacrez. I believe this type of coverage fosters a culture of social media justice where everyone feels empowered to be judge, jury and executioner. Vigilantism isn't just for tween boys turning into super heroes any more.

What happens when we are done shaming racists, though? Are homophobes next? Misogynists? When those people have all been called out, do we come down on milder misanthropes? Or maybe even parking scofflaws? Is this just what we do now as so-called respectable members of society?

> "A fundamental principle of online-
> shaming is that the process robs
> people of the context that makes
> them human beings."

Insensitive Tweets Can Cause a Tremendous Backlash

Jesse Singal

In the following viewpoint, we meet Monica Foy, a Texas college student who expressed a controversial and insensitive view on Twitter in the wake of a brutal murder of a police officer. While Foy believed her tweet contained an important anti-racist message, supporters of law enforcement disagreed and quickly pounced on her comments. Within hours, she received multiple death threats and was even arrested for a previous offense, for which she had an outstanding warrant. The article questions whether personal context and subtle shades of political meaning can be expressed in 140 characters. Jesse Singal is a New York–based journalist currently working as a senior editor at New York *magazine's website.*

"Monica Foy, the Victim of a Terrifying Right-Wing Internet-Shaming, Speaks Out," Jesse Singal, *New York*, September 4, 2015. Reprinted by permission.

As you read, consider the following questions:

1. What was Monica Foy trying to articulate with her tweet?
2. What life events provided the context for Foy's anger about how certain victims are represented in the media?
3. How did this case intersect with the Black Lives Matter movement?

Tuesday morning felt normal to Monica Foy, a junior and English major at Sam Houston State University. The first thing the 26-year-old, who lives outside Houston with her husband, did when she woke up was check her Twitter and Facebook feeds. Both were full of people mourning the loss of Darren Goforth, a Harris County Sheriff's deputy who was murdered Friday night by a man named Shannon J. Miles, who came up behind him at a gas station, shot him in the back of the head, and then emptied every bullet in his gun into the officer. (No one has identified a motive, but the Houston *Chronicle* reported that Miles has a history of psychiatric illness.)

Foy felt terrible about the shooting, she explained to Daily Intelligencer in the first full interview she has granted after a terrifying few days, but as a politically active person who had been watching with interest and sympathy as the Black Lives Matter movement has grown, she was also bothered by what she saw as a double standard on display in the aftermath of Goforth's death: When an unarmed person of color is killed by police, she said, there's often an immediate effort to prove that they were "no angel," that in some way or another they had it coming (though George Zimmerman was a neighborhood watch volunteer rather than a police officer, this general tendency toward victim-blaming tendency was pretty clearly on display in the case of Trayvon Martin). When a white person—especially a police officer—is killed, people seem much more able to accept the fact that some killings are simply unjustified, full-stop.

So Foy tweeted a dry joke about what she saw as the different ways society responds to different deaths: "I can't believe so many people care about a dead cop and NO ONE has thought to ask what he did to deserve it. He had creepy perv eyes …"

Viewed after the fact, this was clearly an inopportune context in which to make this point—not to mention an insensitive and offensive way to make it. But to Foy, it was an observation she was making privately—she had maybe 20 Twitter followers at the time, and about half of those were family. "I never would write anything like that on Facebook, which is why I have a Twitter account," she said. "I wrote it there because I knew that no one would see it. That's something that I knew that morning. There was no hashtag, I did not mention the deputy by name, I did not say Houston, I did not say anything specific at all."

Disastrously for Foy, the tweet quickly got screen-grabbed and began spreading among right-wing Twitter users, who immediately sought to amplify it. It found its way to Brandon Darby, managing director of Breitbart Texas, part of the far-right Breitbart website. Darby, as he would soon explain, quickly decided that it was on him to step in and defend the murdered deputy's legacy against the threat apparently posed to it by a college student's tweet. And as a journalist with a good-size megaphone, there was one obvious way to do that.

Darby directly informed Foy what was in store for her [tweeting] "You have no idea how much you will regret having been this cold. Enjoy the coming fame!"

Foy didn't understand who Darby was or the sort of platform he had. "I was like, *Yeah, right—good luck*," she said. "I just didn't take it seriously." Meanwhile, the first round of Twitter harassment started in earnest during her drive to school with her husband as various right-wing users caught wind of her tweet and came after her for it. "I started reading some of the comments out loud to my husband, and we laughed about it," Foy said. "We didn't think anything of it—we just thought it was going to be an isolated thing where people say dumb stuff, and that would be it." But when she arrived at school at around 8:30 a.m., she checked her phone again and saw that her mentions "had just exploded." That was when she decided to take the tweet down, and when she noticed that it was being posted to a number of right-wing websites.

Things were about to get much worse. Darby followed through on his threat, publishing a brief article on Breitbart about Foy's tweet, describing her as a "Houston area #BlackLivesMatter supporter"—a reference to the fact that a half-hour before her tweet about the murder, she had published another one consisting solely of the hashtag. The Breitbart writer linked directly to Foy's Facebook and Twitter profiles and mentioned that she was a Sam Houston State University student. "Foy deleted the tweet after numerous individuals began criticizing her on the social media platform," Darby noted. (I emailed Darby some questions about why he saw Foy as a legitimate target, and I got back a response from a Breitbart spokesperson who said that Darby's article was part of the website's ongoing effort to investigate the "violent" nature of BLM and its followers. The response is hard to take seriously given that Foy couldn't be further from a public BLM figure, and that Darby openly admitted to a more straightforward motive: He was furious about the tweet and wanted to bring Foy "fame" among Breitbart readers as retribution.)

For the initial phase of the explosion that followed, Foy was offline: The first round of Twitter notifications had drained her phone's battery, and she had class anyway, so she kept it off from 10:30 a.m. to 3:30 p.m., shortly after she got out of class. "For the most part, I just put it to the back of my head, because I was in class and that was my main concern," she said.

But while Foy was in class, Darby got his wish: The story almost immediately went viral, leading to what can only be described as an epic and scary [s###storm]. Her Facebook and Twitter feeds were inundated with threats and harassment. On the Breitbart website and Facebook page, the number of comments ballooned; there are now more than 41,000. A huge number of the tweets and comments ridiculed her physical appearance, and there was a racially aggrieved undercurrent to many of them: There was frequent speculation about Foy (who looks and identifies as white) sleeping with black men, as well as some comments hoping that she got raped by one.

When Foy got back online after class, she said, "That's when I knew I was FUBAR." She tried to figure out how to turn off notifications on her account or make it private altogether, but couldn't. So the notifications kept coming in, a "constant vibration" as she drove from school to her husband's office to figure out what to do. "It was kind of surreal," she explained, "and I was kind of displaced from the situation, almost. I felt like an outside party watching it happen, I didn't really feel hurt by the comments because it just felt like they're ghosts—it wasn't people that I know, that I'm friends with, or that I see in my community or care about their opinion of me." The individual abusive comments didn't bother her, she said, but rather the galloping speed at which new tweets were arriving, and the sense that she had no way to make them stop.

***

A fundamental principle of online-shaming is that the process robs people of the context that makes them human beings. The whole point is to take a snapshot of someone at their most vulnerable, at their most clueless or seemingly callous, and broadcast that as far and wide as possible. As Jon Ronson explains in his book *So You've Been Publicly Shamed*, when you dig into the story of the target, there's inevitably some bit of nuance that casts the offending remark in a different light.

In the case of Justine Sacco, who was victimized by a worldwide shaming mob after a tweet of hers went viral while she was on a plane to South Africa, it turned out that her remark about the difference in AIDS rates between white and black people was a lame attempt at edgy, *South Park*–ish humor. In the case of a pair of women who posted a Facebook photo of themselves flipping the bird at Arlington National Cemetery, leading to a right-wing mob similar to the one targeting Foy, it turned out that they had an inside joke of taking silly photos in front of signs—it didn't even occur to them that they were insulting deceased veterans. This sort of context is vital to understanding that there's usually a longer, more complicated story behind the remarks that spark these incidents than "The person who posted this is evil incarnate."

Foy's case echoes Sacco's in certain ways—she was making a politically incorrect remark about a tragic subject (and was offline for a portion of the phase when the outrage first ramped up). But her broader fixation on the problem of victim-blaming stems from something that happened when she was a teenager. "I went to a really racially charged high school," she said. Her junior year, a Mexican-American student in her class named David Ritcheson—"somewhere between an acquaintance and a friend, since we were also neighbors," she said—was invited to a party by a girl, and was then viciously attacked. "Four or five skinheads—self-claimed skinheads—beat him unconscious, dragged his body outside, sodomized him, poured broken glass down his throat, and bleached his skin. He was in intensive care for the remainder of the school year. He came back our senior year and you could tell that while he was there—we voted him prom king, and he had a great girlfriend and supportive friends, and he was a football player and had people supporting him … he was still dead inside. He wasn't the same person, obviously, after coming back from something like that. And the summer after we graduated, he jumped off a cruise ship and killed himself." The attack gained such notoriety that it has its own Wikipedia page, and two teens were sentenced to lengthy prison terms for their role in the attack, which was sparked when the attackers heard that Ritcheson had tried to kiss a 12-year-old girl.

Foy was an Air Force Junior ROTC cadet at the time, and she says she "distinctly" remembers that "a lot of conservative people, military-raised and that sort of thing, wanted to blame" Ritcheson for the attack. "Because they're like, *Why was he there talking to a younger girl?*" That stuck with Foy: Even in the case of an unspeakable, torture-fueled hate crime, there were people rushing to say the victim had brought it upon himself. "I was ostracized for defending him and saying it was sick that anybody would blame the victim, and I distinctly remember my colonel telling me, *Why do you care? Is that your drug dealer or something?* And I just feel like I've always been on the outside, but I stand by the victims."

None of that means that it was wise for Foy to have made an ironic point about victim-blaming directed toward a police officer who had been tragically murdered just days before, or that people who were offended by it were wrong to be offended. But it helps explain why she posted what she posted. This context, of course, was invisible to the online hordes who by mid-afternoon were not only sending nasty comments to Foy, but also barraging her with death threats.

***

By the time Foy got to her husband's office, she'd received a number of increasingly urgent texts from friends who were worried about her—they'd seen what was going on online, and, not knowing Foy had had her phone off for five hours, had noticed that she wasn't responding. Her phone number and address had been leaked online multiple times, and the death threats had started coming in via Twitter, phone calls, and text messages. Foy and her husband rushed home, grabbed what they could—"I was looking out the window the entire time that we were there"—and headed for Foy's mother's house.

Foy and her husband got to her mom's house about 30 minutes before her mom got home. When she did, they tried to explain to her what had happened, but it went about as well as one might expect, stereotypically, when a millennial tries to explain social media and internet-shaming to a parent. The conversation only lasted about ten minutes. "That's when the cops showed up," said Foy. Apparently, one of the online crusaders attacking Foy had discovered she had an outstanding warrant for a misdemeanor assault charge in 2011, and had tipped off law enforcement (though it's also possible the police themselves had run her name—Foy said people on Twitter told her they were going to forward the offending tweet to law enforcement). The police were there to arrest her.

"The cops didn't mention" her tweet, Foy said. "The arresting officer was the most polite person in the world—like, he had grandmother qualities about him. So gentle. When we were in the car, I was in the backseat, and I was like, *Officers, I just want to take the opportunity to tell you how twisted my words got, and how much I support you, and I would never condone killing an officer or another person, ever ...* They took it very well, they were really welcoming to the apology, and they were just completely professional about it. They weren't passive-aggressive or anything."

As Foy was standing at the counter at the jail, getting booked, she said she heard an officer, busy with other tasks, take a phone call on speakerphone. At the other end of the line was the voice of a man she recognized from an earlier voice-mail. First, he asked to speak to an officer who apparently didn't exist, then he asked, "Was that Twitter chick arrested yet?" The officer quickly picked up the phone and took it into another room. "So obviously the [officers] knew about the tweet, but they just played it off really cool when they were with me," said Foy.

A couple hours later, Foy was bailed out, but by then her mom's address had also been posted online (Foy said she also heard of Facebook plans to organize a protest at her mom's place), so she and her husband had to move to a second safe house.

***

The abuse extended to anyone with a visible connection to Foy. Foy's sister, a law student, reported to her that the dean of her law school had gotten angry emails and voice-mails.

So it's no surprise that Foy's university, Sam Houston State, which is known for its criminal-justice program, itself became a target.

The university's initial response didn't necessarily help matters. It issued two statements: The first, by Steven Keating, assistant director of marketing and communication, explained that Foy's tweet would be "evaluated" to see if she had violated the school's

Code of Conduct. The next day, the university's president, Dana Gibson, issued a lengthier statement of her own in which she reaffirmed the university's support for law enforcement. At a time when it was plainly obvious to anyone who was watching that yes, Foy had said something very offensive, but that she was also being inundated with hate and death threats by an online mob, Keating wrote that the university "appreciates the enormous public response in support of law enforcement," while Gibson wrote: "It's reassuring to see how much pride emerges when the Sam Houston name is called into question, and I am heartened to see so many people stand up for law enforcement." (Neither an email to the university's communications shop nor a voice-mail left with Keating were returned.)

Foy said she feels like the university very much has her back, though, based on her offline communications with administrators. "I know that they were extremely pressured to make a statement, and that statement was saying that they would investigate the tweet and they didn't condone violence at all. And I just felt like if I were the university, I would have said that, too." She said that the dean of student life has confirmed to her that the university isn't going to look into disciplinary action. "I've actually gotten an outpouring of support, saying anything I needed from them—they've given me several different numbers, several different outlets. In their eyes, as a student, I'm exonerated." She plans to return to school on Tuesday, and while she says she "might feel a little worried" when she walks by the school's criminal-justice building, overall she has a good support network in place. She said professors have reached out to her and have helped her develop safety plans in the event anything happens on campus. Multiple people have offered to escort her from class to class, in fact, and have given her their personal cell-phone numbers in case she ever feels unsafe and needs someone to talk to. (Thursday, Foy issued an apology via a statement she sent to the *Chronicle*.)

The bigger threat probably comes from beyond SHSU, though, and it stems from the difference between run-of-the mill anger about a stranger's behavior, which dissipates relatively quickly, and obsession, which lingers. "A lot of people are angry, and they have a right to be, because, you know, a guy was pumping gas in his uniform and he got shot 15 times in the back of the head, and that's fucked-up," said Foy. The problem is that she appears to have picked up some rather dedicated harassers and stalkers, like the guy who both called her at home and called the police. "I don't know what they don't have going on in their lives that they have so much time to do that, but that's what they fill their time with." Whatever motivates them, Foy said she takes their threats very seriously. "You can tell a person's affect from the way they speak, and you can tell they're just not stable."

Thursday, for the first time since the tweet, Foy didn't get a single death threat. But she said she woke up Friday to two new voice-mails again threatening her life. "I don't think I'll ever feel safe again," Foy said, simply because a small percentage of the people who attacked her seem so unhinged. "To the majority of the public it'll blow over. Labor Day weekend's coming up, and I know people are going to party and forget. But there is a percentage of people that—I'm on their list. I'm on their eternal list, and they want my head on the chopping block." It's a numbers thing, in other words. "It just takes one bullet to kill me from one gun from one person, and that one person is out there. So no, I will never feel safe. Not for me, not for my family, not for anyone I know who has publicly supported me."

(Update: This article originally implied that George Zimmerman was a police officer rather than a neighborhood watch volunteer. The language has been updated to accurately describe his position at the time of Trayvon Martin's death.)

> *"The politics of social-media shaming might seem complex, but they're remarkably simple."*

Social Media Shaming Is a Good Thing

Matt Buchanan

In the following viewpoint, Matt Buchanan argues that those who are shamed on social media get what they deserve. According to the author, if you violate the social contract against hateful and offensive speech, you deserve no mercy. Furthermore, Buchanan notes that sites such as Twitter are public forums. Thus one cannot say that the offensive line was meant for a limited audience, since it is posted on a public forum. This is tantamount to holding a sign in public. If shaming goes too far, that may be unfortunate, but the author takes the minority opinion that those who post hurtful comments deserve whatever wrath they incur. Matt Buchanan is a writer for Buzzfeed, the Awl, and others.

As you read, consider the following questions:

1. What is the author's position on social media shaming?
2. What qualities of social media does the author point out that back up his point of view?
3. How might the author counter claims that shaming goes too far?

"Why Social-Media Shaming Is Ok," Matt Buchanan, Buzzfeed, November 13, 2012. Reprinted by permission.

W hen Internet archaeologists look back at 2012 and talk about fleeting micro-cottage industries on the Web—GIFs!—the one that'll have inevitably stuck is our own current form of Twitter archaeology, unearthing and displaying the worst of humanity in very near real time.

Here's how it works: A thing happens. Say, a black president is reelected. People react, many on Facebook and Twitter. Thanks to the sheer, quaking scale of these networks—a billion and 160 million users, respectively—inevitably some slice of that vast chunk of humanity says deeply stupid or aggressively awful things. Websites (like BuzzFeed!) collect and exhibit these stunning little snippets of speech. Internet audiences gather to mock and shame. Wash, rinse, repeat.

The politics of social-media shaming might seem complex, but they're remarkably simple: When people say things out loud that the public has collectively—or like, a lot of it, anyway—agreed are offensive, hurtful, or stupid, it's within the purview of the public to retort, to challenge, and to chasten. That's the one price of creating public speech: When you open your (metaphorical) mouth and project things into the public sphere, you are inviting the public to say something back. And Facebook updates, tweets, and Tumblr posts, unless they're locked behind a private account, are public speech.

There's counterargument to this, but it's wholly incorrect:

> Users have a right to know what is happening with their communication, and they don't have to participate in surveys, research, or even in media articles if they don't want to. Sometimes communication between friends really is just communication between friends. Collecting their data could even be a copyright violation.

The Twitter terms of use, for instance, are quite clear in this, even providing helpful plain-English translations of what you're agreeing to when you use Twitter: "This license is you authorizing us to make your Tweets available to the rest of the world and to let others do the same." Further, Twitter says, "We encourage and permit broad re-use of Content." Twitter even has a feature that specifically allows sites to embed users' tweets, just like a YouTube video. If people don't want their speech to be subject to criticism, they shouldn't post it on social networks specifically designed to be broadcast media.

While online identity over the last several years has been marked by the steady application of real names and real faces to previously anonymous personas in more and more places on the Web—this is not news, whether you're 12 or 72—there does seem to have been a shift in the last year or so in which not only are real people tied to the things that they say and do online, but they're *responsible* for them. And it's this application of moral weight to previously amoral spaces that's behind the rise of name-and-shame posting and the "doxxing" of the Web's most notorious trolls, like Michael Brutsch and Shashank Tripathi. You might be able to say and do these things anonymously, but increasingly, you incur the risk that you will be exposed.

This was inevitable: You start using real names and making real people out of bits, then all of the other things we deal with as people in the real world naturally begin to seep into the online world as well—like moral sensibilities. Now that the Internet is less and less a distinct, separate space from the rest of our lives—at least for most of us, it's just how we live—the consensus is rapidly crystalizing that the rules and sensibilities of the rest of our lives should largely apply online as well. This is simply where we are in 2012.

After all, why should this woman be allowed to be violently offensive and hopelessly ignorant, just because she's doing so on the Internet? If there is no shame in what she posted, why delete the post? Or an entire social media presence, as many of the people featured in the post have? We've decided these people largely don't belong in public life in the real world, so why should we tolerate them on the Internet?

The question, then, isn't whether websites and the online public should be allowed to name and shame the most virulently racist

Shame as an Industry

A medium that demands instant responses and opinions—on subjects we often know little or nothing about—has succeeded in creating a culture of seemingly constant outrage. Despite the fact that our industry is bursting with self-appointed experts in social media, a plethora of brands, individuals and businesses are finding themselves in the firing line on an almost daily basis.

For individuals caught up in the shame culture, the stakes are much higher. It is no exaggeration to say that we live in an age when people have been "shamed to death" by trolls. [Monica] Lewinsky argues that we are all complicit in this exchange; that the shame generates clicks and advertising dollars, which fuel the empathy crisis.

She explains: "Cruelty to others is nothing new, but online, technologically advanced shaming is amplified, uncontained and permanently accessible. The echo of embarrassment used to extend only as far as your family, village or community, but now it extends online across the world."

Social media may have given us all a voice, but the industry is at risk of promoting a "fight or flight" response to any given crisis. In our rush to shame, humiliate and call out any perceived indiscretion, we risk diminishing ourselves in the process.

"The social media bloodsport of public shaming has big implications for brands," Nicola Kemp, Campaign, June 4, 2015.

and sexist amongst us—answer: a clear, unambiguous yes—but how far they should go in exacting moral rectitude. It's simply a matter of taste. For instance, we removed four of the accounts that tweeted about assassinating the president from this post upon request, but I don't think we were under any obligation to do so. For contrast, there's Jezebel's envelope-pushing expose of teenagers who said racist things about the president: Jezebel didn't simply round up and display their tweets for the rhetorical public beating they deserved, the post's author tracked down the students and *reported them to school administrators.*

This is the kind of thing that Gawker Media excels at—taking something that's only recently acceptable and torquing it just enough to push the boundaries of taste, precisely to expose how fragile those boundaries are. In this case, by focusing exclusively on minors and by exacting consequences in the real world for racist online speech. It reeks of stunt vigilantism—largely because it is—but the fact remains that these students, using their real names and real faces, intentionally said deeply offensive things in public. It's no different than if they had stood in a public park holding up a sign as TV cameras rolled by—that's essentially what Twitter is, as a written record. And there are consequences for thinking and saying these kinds of things, particularly in a society that is increasingly liberal. (What I would've done if I had written that post: told the kids' parents, not the school.)

There is perhaps a kind of magical thinking happening here that should be corrected: Teenagers are more keenly aware than anybody how the Internet works, particularly amongst their own social circles, but in the tweets highlighted by Jezebel there is a strange sense that whatever they say lacks any sense of real consequence because it's the Internet. Which is a typical teenage behavior in a sense—you understand a lot of things, just not *consequences*. But asking everyone to persistently pretend this stuff doesn't exist doesn't only ignore how the Internet works, it ignores a greater sense of how the world should be, where these things don't belong. Also, focusing exclusively on the minors question makes us lose sight of the broader point: Racism and sexism shouldn't be left alone simply because they're occurring inside of a chat bubble.

The Internet is real. More real than it's ever been, in a sense. And when you say things on the Internet now, they carry real weight and meaning. That evolution is a good thing, mostly. But reality has a price, and it is consequence. If you didn't know that already, you should now.

Periodical and Internet Sources Bibliography

The following articles have been selected to supplement the diverse views presented in this chapter.

Caitlin Dewey, "Censorship, Fat-Shaming and the 'Reddit revolt': How Reddit Became the Alamo of the Internet's Ongoing Culture War," *Washington Post*, June 12, 2015. https://www .washingtonpost.com/news/the-intersect/wp/2015/06/12/ censorship-fat-shaming-and-the-reddit-revolt-how-reddit -became-the-alamo-of-the-internets-ongoing-culture-war.

Peter DeWitt, "Social Media: Is It Today's Modern Day Public-Shaming Venue?" *Education Week*, July 29, 2015. http://blogs .edweek.org/edweek/finding_common_ground/2015/07/social_ media_is_it_todays_modern_day_public_shaming_venue.html.

Todd Leopold, "The Price of Public Shaming in the Internet Age," CNN, April 16, 2015. http://edition.cnn.com/2015/04/16/living/ feat-public-shaming-ronson.

Diana Moukalled, "The Perils of Social Media's Public Shaming," Al Arabiya English, August 5, 2015. http://english.alarabiya.net/en/ views/news/middle-east/2015/08/05/The-perils-of-social-media -s-public-shaming.html.

Joan Williams and Katherine Ullman, "Is It Too Cold to 'Lean In'? Women in STEM," Huffington Post, April 12, 2013. http://www. huffingtonpost.com/joan-williams/is-it-too-cold-to-lean -in_b_3055759.html.

OPPOSING
VIEWPOINTS®
SERIES

CHAPTER 4

Is Public Shaming an Appropriate Means of Punishing Criminal Offenders?

Chapter Preface

Public shaming has re-entered the judicial arena with a vengeance. In a bygone era, the courts routinely harnessed the power of public shame to humiliate the offending person in the eyes of the community. As a society, we have largely determined that displays of thieves in stocks on the village square are cruel spectacles unfit for modern life. More to the point, it does not work: as urbanization and industrialization dissolved traditional social bonds, the power of shame to deter crime has diminished. In other words, since we no longer know our neighbor particularly well, we probably do not worry much about their opinion.

Of course, the internet and social media now have the power to profoundly shift this dynamic. In the past, only those in the local community would see the result of a public shaming punishment. Now, a photo can go viral and expose an individual to the scorn and vitriol of millions. While this is potentially humiliating, questions remain as to whether this is the direction our criminal justice system should be moving. Should the law be held to higher standards of decency, or are these standards simply evolving before our eyes?

Emboldened by such possibilities, more and more judges are bucking their reputation as black-robed, stodgy arbiters of justice by meting out novel punishments that do not rely on typical sentencing guidelines such as jail or monetary fines. Such punishment has almost always been upheld as constitutional. Moreover, there is much temptation, and some good reason, for judges to hand out these punishments. Prison is notoriously burdensome on society, as each inmate costs taxpayers tens of thousands of dollars annually. Critics of the prison system also point out that it is not a terribly effective means of rehabilitation. In fact, one hallmark of jail is that it often brings a casual offender into deeper contact with gangs and other elements of the illegal world. Requiring a thief to hold a sign announcing his transgression may be much better for society overall, given this reality.

Despite some superficial appeal, public shaming has several downsides as a form of criminal justice. It is unpredictable in scope and may be disproportionate for that reason. Also, it can expose the criminal to unintended danger or retaliation. Judges who do not wish to encourage vigilante justice are advised to avoid this temptation. Nonetheless, some court publicity and notoriety for political or personal gain. While there is no doubt this approach to justice grabs attention, whether it is in fact justice is debatable.

"*Experts say it stands to reason that so long as the public is entertained by shaming sentences, they will continue to be imposed.*"

Judges Should Not Use Public Shaming for Publicity's Sake

David M. Reutter

In the following viewpoint, David Reutter chronicles the recent trend among judges to impose creative and humiliating shame-based punishment instead of traditional sentences such as prison and fines. Using expert opinions to bolster his position, Reutter argues that these novel punishments are ineffective crime deterrents and may also raise questions about fairness and civil rights. Moreover, Reutter is concerned that judges may be using novel shame tactics to blur the line between justice and entertainment, often for their own aggrandizement and political gain. On the other hand, he notes the appeal of these punishments, particularly since prison is costly and badly in need of reform. David M. Reutter is a writer and regular contributor to Prison Legal News.

"For Shame! Public Shaming Sentences On the Rise," David M. Reutter, *Prison Legal News,* February 4, 2015. Reprinted by permission.

As you read, consider the following questions:

1. Why do some people argue that prison is worse than public shaming?
2. What is legal expert Jonathan Turley's main concern with unique shaming punishments?
3. How might court-sanctioned public shaming punishments be discriminatory?

Punishments intended to shame offenders for wrongdoing, popular throughout history, are once again on the rise—particularly as penalties imposed by judges who enjoy seeing their names in the newspaper or on television due to their "creative" sentencing practices.

Whether judges hand down sentences that humiliate defendants for the purpose of entertainment, self-aggrandizement or as a unique way of deterring crime with a "punishment that fits" is subject to debate. The only certainty is that most sanctions designed to shame offenders are legal, so long as judges do not go too far.

Shaming criminals has long been an integral part of America's criminal justice system, and public whipping and the stocks were commonly used in Puritan and colonial times. During that era, imprisonment was reserved for debtors and those awaiting trial; upon conviction, a judge could order an offender to be executed, flogged, banished or shamed.

"While the sentences recognize hope for the individual, they can also be dehumanizing," said Professor Mark Osler of the St. Thomas University of Law.

Indeed, that was the intent of one colonial judge who sentenced a man convicted of stealing a pair of pants. The judge ordered him to sit in the stocks with "a pair of breeches about his necke." Public shaming sentences began to fade around the time of the American Revolution, though some shaming punishments, such as the pillory and branding for horse thieves, continued into the 1800s.

Urbanization and migration, say historians, undermined the use of public shaming because people no longer feared the condemnation of their communities. Imprisonment became the punishment of choice, yet states like Pennsylvania and Massachusetts still tried to shame prisoners by allowing the public to watch them "as if in a zoo."

Some argue that the current system of incarcerating criminals and then releasing them on parole, or placing them on probation, is nothing more than a modern version of shaming. Critics of the criminal justice system contend that, like a yoke around the neck, criminal records follow former offenders forever, often preventing them from obtaining suitable employment, housing and public services.

"The purpose of incarceration ironically is to make someone feel ashamed at the end," said Peter Moskos, an associate professor of law and political science at the City University of New York, in a debate on shaming punishments that aired on National Public Radio (NPR) in August 2013. "We just have this horrible middle process to get someone there and we want people to feel shame and see what they did was wrong."

Moskos, who authored the book *In Defense of Flogging*, said the idea of humiliating punishments is to give people convicted of minor offenses an alternative to prison. "It's not that I want to see people whipped, but ... if you're sentenced to five years in prison for whatever you did or didn't do, and the judge gave you the choice of ten lashes, what would you pick?

"Almost everyone would choose the lashes, but we don't allow that because we consider it cruel and unusual. But if it's better than prison, what does that say about the system we have?" he concluded.

Jonathan Turley, a professor of public interest law at George Washington University Law School, said during the NPR debate that he agrees that the current prison system is in need of reform but disagrees about shaming punishments.

"Let's reform our prisons. Let's focus on that," he stated. "But to say that we should go to a Singapore flogging system is breathtaking. We did that. We were there. We had flogging posts in [and] around our cities and towns. It was an extremely dark and medieval period."

Shaming punishments "have really undermined the quality and character of justice in this country," Turley added. "That is, it allows judges to become little Caesars that make citizens perform demeaning acts and shaming acts."

However, at least one state lawmaker thinks there's merit in public flogging. Montana Rep. Jerry O'Neil said he crafted legislation that would give convicted offenders the ability to choose between prison or the "infliction of physical pain."

"Ten years in prison or you could take 20 lashes, perhaps two lashes a year? What would you choose?" Rep. O'Neil said.

"It is actually more moral than we do now," he added. "I think it's immoral to put someone in prison for a long time, to take them away from their family, and force that family to go on welfare."

The idea was widely criticized by other Montana lawmakers and the American Civil Liberties Union, and O'Neil's bill, LC1452, died in committee in April 2013.

The advent of mass media that seeks to entertain more than inform has contributed to the growing popularity of public shaming, and has helped some judges—who garner attention by imposing such sentences—become so popular that they have their own TV shows. For example, a Memphis judge allowed the victims of a theft to enter the thief's house and take anything they wanted as neighbors watched. The notoriety of that shaming sentence helped make Judge Joe Brown a household name for those who watch reality court TV.

The "King of Shame," Harris County, Texas state judge Ted Poe, felt "people have too good a self-esteem." To bring defendants who appeared in his court down a rung, he would order them to do such things as shovel manure. While those punishments had little to do with justice, they did help Poe secure a Congressional seat in 2004, and he remains in Congress today.

While studies show that shaming sentences are a poor deterrent to crime, the publicity surrounding such punishments makes them popular choices for judges who thrive on public attention. Then there are judges, such as Georgia's Russell "Rusty" Carlisle, who apparently enjoy humiliating people. When a littering defendant seemed "kind of cocky," Carlisle ordered him to use a butter knife to scrape gum off courtroom benches.

"The shaming punishments that we have seen are comical. They are ludicrous," Professor Turley noted. He said some judges ignore valid sentencing alternatives in order to seek notoriety. "It is a corruptive element in our judicial system and from what we've seen from judges is it's completely corrupting in terms of their own judgment and their own conduct," he stated. "They get worse and worse to get into the headlines."

Judges have imposed a variety of shaming sentences in recent years, including:

- In November 2012, Shena Hardin, who was caught on camera passing a school bus by driving on a sidewalk, was ordered by Cleveland, Ohio Municipal Court Judge Pinkey Carr to stand at an intersection wearing a sign that read, "Only an idiot would drive on the sidewalk to avoid a school bus." Similarly, in March 2013, Carr sentenced another defendant, Richard Dameron, who had threatened police officers, to stand outside a police station for three hours a day for one week with a sign apologizing to the officers and stating "I was being an idiot and it will never happen again." Dameron failed to show up to hold the sign and was sentenced to 90 days in jail.
- In April 2014, Ohio Municipal Court Judge Gayle Williams-Byer ordered defendant Edmond Aviv to remain on a street corner for five hours with a sign that read, "I AM A BULLY! I pick on children that are disabled, and I am intolerant of those that are different from myself. My actions do not reflect an appreciation for the diverse South Euclid community that I live in." Aviv had pleaded no contest to disorderly

conduct for harassing a neighboring family. "This isn't fair at all," he complained.

- A Georgia judge gave Natasha Freeman, 38, a choice of spending four weekends in jail or wearing a sign to resolve charges related to her boarding a school bus to assault her 11-year-old cousin. Freeman chose to wear a sign that said, "I made a fool out of myself on a Bibb County Public Schools bus" for one week, starting on December 10, 2012.

- In 2008, Cleveland, Ohio Housing Court Judge Ray Pianka ordered landlord Nicholas Dionisopoulos to live in one of his own rental properties for six months after he was found in violation of multiple building codes. He also had to pay a $100,000 fine.

- In May 2012, a judge in Utah imposed the same punishment on two girls, 11 and 13, that they had inflicted on a 3-year-old girl they befriended at McDonald's. The older girls cut the little girl's hair into a bob with a pair of dollar store scissors. The judge sentenced the 13-year-old to detention and 276 hours of community service, but gave her the option to reduce the community service by more than half if she had her hair cut in the courtroom. She agreed. The 11-year-old was ordered to have her hair cut short at a salon.

- Two days before Christmas in 2013, Montana District Judge G. Todd Baugh ordered Pace Anthony Ferguson, 27, to write "Boys do not hit girls" 5,000 times as part of his punishment for punching his girlfriend. Ferguson was also ordered to serve six months in jail and pay $3,800 in medical bills for fracturing the woman's face in three places.

- In Pennsylvania, a prosecutor told two women to submit to public humiliation or face charges for stealing from a child. Evelyn Border, 55, and her daughter, Tina Griekspoor, 35, were caught taking a gift card from a girl at Wal-Mart in 2009. They chose to stand in front of the courthouse holding signs that read, "I stole from a 9-year-old on her birthday! Don't steal or this could happen to you." The girl, Marissa Holland, reportedly said, "I think it's pretty fair. They deserved it. I want them to feel sorry."

- Daniel and Eloise Mireles, convicted of stealing from a victims' fund in Harris County, Texas in 2010, were sentenced to a lengthy humiliating sentence. Along with jail terms, community service and restitution, the Mireleses were ordered by Judge Kevin Fine to hold signs saying "I am a thief" at a busy intersection every weekend for six years. They also were required to post a sign in front of their house that included their names and said they were convicted thieves.

- A Wisconsin man who crashed his car into the gates of a wastewater treatment plant while drunk in 2008 was forced to choose between 20 days in jail for criminal damage to property or to stand at the plant for eight hours with a sign that said, "I was stupid." He chose the sign.

- After Jonathan Tarase pleaded no contest to DUI in January 2013, Painesville, Ohio Municipal Court Judge Michael Cicconetti, who is known for his unusual sentences, gave him a choice of either serving five days in jail or viewing the bodies of two victims killed in car accidents and taking a substance abuse course. In January 2014, Judge Cicconetti ordered Jeffrey Gregg to complete 400 hours of community service—while wearing a Santa Claus hat. Gregg's offense? He had posed as a Salvation Army bell ringer to collect money for himself. "It is too easy to put people in jail," Cicconetti said. "They go to jail and ... it does not deter the crime."

The above examples are in addition to more widespread public shaming of offenders both before they are convicted—such as booking mugshots posted by jails, and police websites that display photos of defendants arrested for soliciting prostitutes—and post-conviction shaming that includes sex offender registries, which have become ubiquitous.

Nor are modern shaming sentences a recent trend; in 2003, a Texas man was ordered to spend 30 consecutive nights in a 2-by-3 foot doghouse for whipping his stepson with a car antenna.

The judge did allow Curtis Robin, Sr. to have a sleeping bag, mosquito netting, plastic tarp or similar items during his stint in the doghouse. Other more recent sentences designed to shame or humiliate offenders have been reported since the 1990s.

Not all shaming sentences are legal or constitutional, though; some are questionable. For example, a 27-year-old Virginia man agreed in June 2014 to undergo a surgical vasectomy in order to reduce his prison sentence for child endangerment, stemming from a vehicle accident that caused minor injuries to one of his children. "He needs to be able to support the children he already has when he gets out," said prosecutor Ilona White, who admitted the offer was intended to prevent Jessie Lee Herald from fathering more children than the seven he already had with at least six women.

"This takes on the appearance of social engineering," complained Richmond, Virginia attorney Steve Benjamin, past president of the Virginia Association of Criminal Defense Lawyers. "Sentencing conditions are designed to prevent future criminal behavior," he said. "Fathering children is not criminal behavior."

In Oklahoma, District Court Judge Mike Norman ordered Tyler Alred, 17, to attend church for 10 years as a condition of his sentence for DUI manslaughter. Alred was behind the wheel of a pickup truck that crashed in December 2011, killing a passenger. The Oklahoma ACLU condemned the sentence, imposed in November 2012, as a "clear violation of the First Amendment," and filed a complaint against Norman. But the judge defended the punishment, which Alred had agreed to. Other conditions of the sentence included requirements that Alred graduate from high school, graduate from welding school, take drug and alcohol tests, and participate in victim impact panels.

Cameron County, Texas Justice of the Peace Gustavo "Gus" Garza allowed parents to spank their children in his courtroom in lieu of paying a fine, for which he was admonished by the State Commission on Judicial Conduct on March 9, 2009. The Commission concluded that "Judge Garza exceeded his authority by providing parents and the school district with a 'safe haven' for the administration of corporal punishment ... with no legal authority to impose the sanction either by the Texas Education Code or Texas Code of Criminal Procedure."

And in Pennsylvania, in August 2014 a Superior Court struck down part of a shaming sentence imposed on former state Supreme Court Justice Joan Orie Melvin, who was convicted of misusing public funds and using court and legislative staff to run her election campaigns. The trial court had ordered her to send pictures of herself wearing handcuffs to judges across the state; the Superior Court wrote that "the handcuffs as a prop is emblematic of the intent to humiliate Orie Melvin in the eyes of her former judicial colleagues.... It was solely intended to shame her."

"Judges have the power to create their own unique sentences. And courts have ruled that sentences involving public shaming are constitutional as long as they aspire to some other goal, such as deterrence or retribution," wrote *Reason* magazine contributing editor Greg Beato. "But equal application of the law is a crucial element of our justice system. It's one of the reasons we have sentencing guidelines. And quirky punishments designed to go viral don't just fail to meet this standard of the law; they actively subvert it. Their primary goal is to court publicity, and that publicity can't be accurately anticipated or controlled."

Experts say it stands to reason that so long as the public is entertained by shaming sentences, they will continue to be imposed. "These are punishments that often appeal to the public and bring a type of instant gratification for the court," said Professor Turley. "To some extent, we've seen the merging of law and entertainment in the last 10 years.

"Most of these people probably would not go to jail," he added. "People aren't taking a murderer and saying, 'I want you to bark like a dog in my courtroom and I'll let you off for murder.' These are relatively small offences and many of them would not result in incarceration or weekend incarceration, but what these judges do is they impose very heavy sentences in order to force people to do what they want."

There may also be socioeconomic bias with respect to shaming sentences—when such punishments are offered as an option in lieu of fines, poor defendants are more inclined to chose them while wealthy offenders who can afford to pay financial penalties are less likely to submit to humiliating sanctions.

Unfortunately, many judges do not seem to understand that they can impose creative sentences that do not result in public shaming. For example, in December 2014 the *Detroit News* reported that Wayne County, Michigan Circuit Court Judge Deborah Thomas, a former teacher, requires defendants to finish high school or obtain a GED certificate as part of their sentences. She posts the diplomas and certificates on her courtroom wall.

"Their job prospects are more limited, they have lower self-esteem," Thomas said of offenders who did not finish high school. "But when they have [the diploma] they have success, they realize 'I can succeed at other things.'" She added, "I tell them just because you came through here doesn't mean this has to be your permanent route.... We punish negative behavior. We should reward positive behavior."

Sources: *Associated Press, www.cbs12.com, www.myfox.com, www.abcnews.go.com, www.slate.com, USA Today, www.foxnews.com, www.wordoncampus.com, Detroit News, www.huffingtonpost.com, www.csmonitor.com, www.correctionsone.com, www.ksl.com, www.npr.org, www.latimes.com, www.local8now.com, www.dailymail.co.uk, http://blog .constitutioncenter.org, http://blogs.findlaw.com, www.cleveland.com, www.reason.com*

*"Shaming...is not reasonably related
to rehabilitation."*

Public Shaming Might Not Constitute Cruel and Unusual Punishment

Lyle Denniston

In this viewpoint, Lyle Denniston takes a look at the increase in public shaming punishments. He claims that it is unclear whether public shaming violates the Eighth Amendment's prohibition on cruel and unusual punishment. Despite considerable leeway offered to judges in meting out specific punishment, at least five state supreme courts have ruled that public shaming does in fact violate the Eighth Amendment in spirit. One such case involved a Pennsylvania judge who was convicted of misappropriating funds and forced to send her picture in handcuffs to former colleagues, among other punishments. The handcuff photo was eventually nullified. Lyle Denniston is a constitutional literacy adviser at the National Constitution Center.

As you read, consider the following questions:

1. Is shaming considered "cruel and unusual" punishment?
2. When are shaming penalties considered justified?
3. Do judges take the attitude and dispositions of both victim and perpetrator into account during sentencing?

"Constitution Check: Is Shaming a Legal Form of Punishment for Crime?" Lyle Denniston, *Constitution Daily,* August 26, 2014. Reprinted by permission.

The Statement at Issue:

"We must conclude that while a sentencing court has wide latitude to design conditions to assist in efforts at rehabilitation, no condition may be imposed for the sole purpose of shaming or humiliating the defendant…We note that the highest courts in at least five sister states have reached similar conclusions, namely that shaming is not reasonably related to rehabilitation and may in many circumstance overshadow any possible rehabilitative effects that the punishment might otherwise provide."

– Excerpt from a decision August 21 by the Pennsylvania Superior Court, nullifying a part of a criminal sentence that required a former state judge to send to all other judges in the state a photograph of herself wearing handcuffs, with an apology for her crimes written on the photo.

We Checked the Constitution, and …

With the Constitution's Eighth Amendment in the background, judges who impose sentences on an individual convicted of a crime are supposed to know that there are limits on the kind of punishment they may mete out. Not many modern forms of criminal sentencing fail the Eighth Amendment test that bans "cruel and unusual punishment," but the underlying sentiment of that provision is intended to impose a continuing restraint on a judge's discretion.

In recent years, though, there has been a noteworthy revival of an ancient but questionable form of punishment: public shaming. Convicted individuals, of course, are no longer required to walk around in public wearing a "scarlet letter," or some other display of their wrongdoing, for all to cast scorn upon them. And no longer do criminals have to have their hands placed in "stocks" in the village square for a rather painful form of public humiliation.

But judges in recent times have fashioned various new forms of shaming, including measures that seek to warn the community at large that someone dangerous is in their midst. A conspicuous example of that, of course, is the requirement that sex offenders' identities and addresses be widely publicized on a public registry. That, in fact, is a federal law, and its constitutionality has gained the approval even of the Supreme Court.

But however justified that particular form of punishment may be, judges are finding other ways of adding to their sentences mandates for convicted individuals to take steps to publicize their misdeeds, often by some form of apology to the victims. Such a mandate is added onto any fine or jail or prison time imposed on the individual, or in place of jail time. Often, the theory is that an apology helps to rehabilitate the individual, by making sure they take personal responsibility for having done wrong.

The practice has grown up in part because there has been a spreading development in the criminal law of showing more sympathy to victims of crime, and, in fact, to give victims an increasing role in shaping the actual forms of punishment to be imposed.

It is possible, though, for this to go too far, and now a Pennsylvania court—echoing decisions by other state courts—has imposed a definite limit. It did so in the high profile prosecution in Pennsylvania of a member of the state Supreme Court, Justice Joan Orie Melvin.

She was convicted in February of last year in Allegheny County Common Pleas Court of misusing public funds and her court staff and the staff of her sister, a member of the state legislature, to help Orie Melvin in two elections for a seat on the state's highest court—unsuccessfully in 2003, successfully in 2009. A jury convicted her of six criminal counts, essentially of abusing the public trust.

When Common Pleas Judge Lester G. Nauhaus of Pittsburgh sentenced Orie Melvin, to serve three years on house arrest, to do public service in a soup kitchen, and to pay a fine, he added additional conditions. Among them: she had to resign from her seat on the state Supreme Court, and was barred from using the title of "Justice," at least for the next three years.

And the judge imposed two requirements for apologies. The first ordered her to write letters of apology to every member of her judicial staff who had done illegal work for her during her election campaigns.

If Judge Nauhaus had stopped there, that part of the sentence would have been considered an entirely appropriate adjunct to her need for rehabilitation (and, indeed, that part was upheld last week by a higher court, the Pennsylvania Superior Court).

But the sentencing judge went further: he ordered Orie Melvin to sit for a photo by a court photographer, showing herself wearing handcuffs. On the photo, which the former judge was required to send to every state judge in Pennsylvania, she was to write her apology for defiling her judicial office.

The sentencing judge apparently was troubled that Orie Melvin had continued to insist that she had done nothing wrong. He told her: "You have consistently refused to accept any responsibility for any of the harm you have done to the people who worked with you, the electoral process, to your colleagues in the judiciary, and, most of all, your family."

In last week's decision partly upholding her challenge to the sentence, the Pennsylvania Superior Court nullified the photo apology, finding it a violation of state sentencing law (Orie Melvin had not raised an Eighth Amendment claim). Calling the photo apology an "unorthodox gimmick," the Superior Court said that "the trial court's use of the handcuffs as a prop is emblematic of the intent to humiliate Orie Melvin in the eyes of her former judicial colleagues….It was solely intended to shame her."

The requirement, the decision added, could not have actually been intended to contribute to Orie Melvin's rehabilitation, but rather was only "another form of punitive sanction—one not authorized under the Sentencing Code." Shaming, it said, is not "reasonably related to rehabilitation," as "the highest courts in at least five other states" had also concluded.

This was not a constitutional decision. But it did infuse the state's Sentencing Code with the caution that unusual—or, as the court put it, "unorthodox"—criminal punishment is to be avoided.

> *"Public shaming is a form of dehumanization, of stigmatizing the offender with a scarlet 'A' or 'yellow star' or passport symbol."*

The Public Shaming of Sensitive Offenses Violates Civil Rights

David Rosen

In the following viewpoint, David Rosen traces the expanded forms of punishment handed out to convicted sex offenders in the United States. Beginning with Megan's Law in 1994, those convicted of a sex offense were required to register with a database to warn neighbors. This registry has expanded, as new passport identifiers impose restrictions on international travel. Although this is ostensibly to protect the public, some contend that such punishments are overbroad, too long lasting, and needlessly severe. Moreover, opponents argue that this is an infringement on civil rights, and as such constitutes public shaming. David Rosen is the author of Sex, Sin & Subversion: The Transformation of 1950s New York's Forbidden into America's New Normal *(Skyhorse, 2015).*

"21st Century Public Shaming," David Rosen, *Counterpunch,* February 19, 2016. Reprinted by permission.

As you read, consider the following questions:

1. How does the author argue that the category of sex offender may be too broad?

2. Why does the author think Megan's Law may violate civil rights?

3. On what basis does the author equate Megan's Law with public shaming?

O n February 8th, Pres. Obama signed the "International Megan's Law to Prevent Demand for Child Sex Trafficking" (H.R. 515), but made no formal public statement to go along with the signing.

The White House issued a press release accompanying the signing of the new law arguing that it accomplishes two goals. First, it empowers the Department of Homeland Security's "Angel Watch Center" and the Department of Justice's "National Sex Offender Targeting Center" to monitor the international travel of registered sex offenders. Second, it requires the Department of State to include a unique identifier—the 21st century scarlet "A"—on passports issued to registered sex offenders.

Some are calling it "the international Scarlet Letter law," recalling Nathaniel Hawthorne's 1850 classic tale. In the novel, the Massachusetts Puritans of the 1640s force a local woman, Hester Prynne, to wear a scarlet "A" on her dress, thus publicly displaying her shame for having engaged in adultery (with the local pastor) and having an out-of-wedlock child.

The International Megan's Law is the first law in U.S. history in which a special symbol will be placed on a citizen's form of personal identification, a passport, to denote that the individual was convicted of a sex crime. Nearly four centuries after the witch trials, in which women were hung for having sex with the devil, those in authority continue to publicly shame people convicted of engaging in unacceptable sexual practices.

The original "Megan's Law" was named for Megan Kanka, a 7-year-old girl who was sexually assaulted and murdered in 1994. She was abused and killed by a young man who lived across the street from the family in Hamilton Township, NJ; he had been convicted in two prior cases of child molestation and spent six years in prison—and nobody in the neighborhood knew of his past.

The New Jersey legislature hurriedly passed the law in 1994 and, in 1996, Pres. Clinton signed a federal version, requiring all states to warn the public of sex offenders or lose federal funding. Today, all 50 states and the District of Columbia enforce a version of the law.

Rep. Chris Smith (R-NJ), the Congressmen from Megan's district, promoted the original law as well as the international version. Under the original law, state governments were required to notify communities when a convicted sex offender moved into a neighborhood. The new version extends notification to foreign countries by monitoring—and sometimes preventing— the international travel of a convicted sex offender. It also requests foreign countries report if any of their convicted sex offenders travel to the U.S. A 2010 Government Accountability Office (GAO) report found that in fiscal year 2008 at least 4,500 registered sex offenders received a U.S. passport.

Sex offender registration preceded Megan's Law. Karne Newburn, in a detailed legal analysis, "The Prospect of an International Sex Offender Registry," carefully lays out the history of such regulation. She points out that the same year New Jersey passed the original Megan's law, 1994, the U.S. Congress passed a law named after Jacob Wetterling, an 11-year-old abducted in St. Joseph, MN, that called for states to voluntarily register convicted sex offenders.

In '96, the Congress enacted the "Pam Lychner Sexual Offender Tracking and Identification Act" requiring the U.S. Attorney General to establish the National Sex Offender Registry and required lifetime registration for certain types of sex offenders. In '98, it extended the legislation to include sexually violent offenders; in 2000, it passed the "Campus Sex Crimes Prevention Act"; and,

THE SHAME OF THE "PERP WALK"

The perp walk has become a staple for prosecutors in high profile cases. The "innocent until proven guilty" mantra of the American criminal justice system has no usefulness in this arena. The history of perp walks goes back to the days of organized crime arrests, where John Gotti turned these events into fashion shows. The process was perfected by Rudy Giuliani, when he was the United States Attorney for the Southern District of New York. With a penchant for drama (and an unabashed political ambition) he raided brokerage houses, trading firms and luxury apartments with the press in tow. Little did he care about those innocent defendants who would take their cases to trial and walk out of the courtroom acquitted. To him, the arrest and the public shame and humiliation became the name of the game.

It's time to end this senseless and unnecessary practice. It unfairly stigmatizes the accused, and places a "GUILTY" scarlet banner across his or her forehead, even before the charges are read to the Judge. It disgraces our criminal justice system and, along with our massive experiment in incarceration, belittles our international reputation.

Carol Argo, "Time to End the "Perp Walk," NCIA.

in 2006, it passed the "Adam Walsh Act" that increased the number of specified sex-crime offenses required for registration.

Newburn details what is involved in "registration." The convicted offender "must provide their names, social security numbers, the name and address of their employers, the name and address of places where they attend school, and the license plate number and description of vehicles they own or operate." The offender's criminal record is also made public, including the dates of any prior arrests, convictions or outstanding warrants as well as parole, probation and supervisory release status. The registration includes a physical description, a current photograph, set of fingerprints, palm prints and a DNA sample.

* * *

In 2014, there were 796,598 people on the national sex offender registry. Unfortunately, while the popular media promotes the image of an isolated male sex predictor ready to strike everywhere at anytime, most sex offenses against children are incestuous acts that take place in a child-care setting, too often the home.

Civil liberties advocates have raised serious reservations about the new law.

Human Rights Watch argues that U.S. "registration laws are overbroad in scope and very long in duration." Chrysanthi Leon, a professor of gender studies at the University of Delaware, argues that registrants are unlikely to commit new sex crimes. More so, she warns, such monitoring could harm members of family who will be blocked from travel.

David Post, writing in *The Washington Post*, took offense at the new legal designation comparing it to the Nazi use of "yellow star" identifying Jews. He sternly insists that this is the first time in U.S. history that a special designation will appear on a citizen's passports. The definition of a sex offender includes anyone previously convicted, at any point in his/her life, of a sex offense.

Janice Bellucci, a civil rights attorney and president of the advocacy group, California Reform Sex Offender Laws, rhetorically argued, "Who is going to have a unique identifier added to their passport next? Is it going to be Muslims? Is it going to be gays?" The group filed a lawsuit in the U.S. District Court in San Francisco challenging the new law.

The true number of people trafficked in the sex trade, especially children and young girls, is difficult to determine. In a 2015 assessment of sex trafficking, "Sex Trafficking of Children in the United States," the Congressional Research Service (CRS) reported that "the exact number of child victims of sex trafficking in the United States is unknown because of challenges in defining the population and varying methodologies used to arrive at estimates."

In 2012, David Finkelhor and Lisa Jones, with the University of New Hampshire's Crimes Against Children Research Center, released an influential study, "Have Sexual Abuse and Physical Abuse Declined Since the 1990s?," noted: "There was a 56% decline in physical abuse and a 62% decline in sexual abuse from 1992 to 2010."

In 2009, Finkelhor, Richard Ormrod and Mark Chaffin found, in a Justice Department study, "Juveniles Who Commit Sex Offenses Against Minors," that more than one-quarter (25.8 percent) of all sex offenders and more than one-third (35.6 percent) of sex offenders against juvenile victims were other juveniles; most of these offenders (93%) were boys between 12 and 14 years of age. These youths are likely registered as sex offenders and swept up by the new law.

Unfortunately, child sexual abuse is widespread. According to one study, in the U.S., 1 in 5 girls and 1 in 20 boys is a victim of child sexual abuse. Some self-reporting studies claim that 20 percent of adult females and 5-10 percent of adult males recall a childhood sexual assault or sexual abuse incident.

The U.S. has come a long way from the Puritan world depicted by Hawthorne in *The Scarlet Letter*. Four centuries ago, violation of the social order was conceived of as a "sin," a moral failing; today, a violation is considered a "crime," a civil offense. Violations include rape, pedophilia, child porn, sex trafficking, infecting with an STD/AIDS and lust murder. Today's moral order is based on a belief in the equality of each participant, no matter which gender, but whether they are rational (i.e., capable of saying No!) and age-appropriate.

Today, those who violate mutual consent are considered immoral, pathological or criminal. And the worst—the most socially stigmatized segment of those who violate sexual consent—is the man (or, far less often, woman) who perpetrates a child sex crime. These crimes include harming the young person through sexual abuse, prostitution, pornography and lust murder.

The International Megan's Law, like the original Megan's Law, is not an act of legal punishment. While the Eighth Amendment bans cruel and unusual punishment, public shaming has deep roots in the American legal system and, according to a 2015 report in *Prison Legal News*, seems to on the increase. Public shaming is a form of dehumanization, of stigmatizing the offender with a scarlet "A" or "yellow star" or passport symbol. The ostensible goal is to prevent the offender from committing another sex crime. However, it's unclear how effective such shaming is in terms of 21st century law enforcement and moral values.

> "In today's technologically driven world, it is possible that the next step for the judiciary would be to incorporate the realm of online social media into its public shaming punishments."

Social Media Shaming Is Fair and Effective Punishment

Lauren M. Goldman

In the following excerpted viewpoint, Lauren Goldman posits a criminal justice system in which the power of social media is harnessed to shame offenders. Critics of public shaming argue that in our era of loosened social bonds, shame has lost its sting as a punishment. However, this may not be true in the era of social media. For example, if a mug shot circulates among an individual's social media world, this would be far from anonymous. According to the author, such punishment would be both legal, defensible, and effective according to legal theories of deterrence, rehabilitation, and incapacitation. Lauren Goldman earned a JD from Georgetown University Law Center.

Lauren M. Goldman, "Trending Now: The Use of Social Media Websites in Public Shaming Punishments," *American Criminal Law Review*, Spring 2015. Reprinted by permission.

As you read, consider the following questions:

1. Why does the author think online public shaming will work for convicted offenders?
2. How would you summarize the legal theories cited to back the author's argument?
3. Are there any potential problems with this approach to criminal justice?

Introduction

Imagine logging into your Facebook account and the first thing you see is a picture of someone you know. Maybe it is a friend from high school or college, perhaps a colleague, a family member, or an acquaintance you have not spoken to for years. This picture is odd because it is unlike a typical Facebook picture of a friend's wedding or a colleague's birthday party: it is that person's mug shot. Alongside the mug shot, the caption reads: "I am a thief. This is my punishment."

At first blush, this scenario seems completely outlandish. However, shaming punishments are alive and well in today's society and are often imposed upon convicts as part of their probation conditions. Courts have yet to take these shaming punishments to the realm of online social media, but such punishments have included other forms of public display[1] and have also infiltrated print media.[2]

In today's technologically driven world, it is possible that the next step for the judiciary would be to incorporate the realm of online social media into its public shaming punishments.

Recently, the Ninth Circuit validated public shaming punishments in *United States v. Gementera*.[3] In *Gementera*, the court upheld the district court's probation condition, which required a twenty-four-year-old convicted mail thief to stand outside of a postal office for eight hours and wear a sandwich board that read: "I stole mail. This is my punishment."[4] Although humiliating, the Ninth Circuit observed that criminal conviction is inherently humiliating.[5] Subsequently, the court of appeals concluded that the district court judge, Judge Vaughn Walker, imposed the condition for the legitimate statutory purposes of rehabilitation, deterrence, and protection of the public, and that the condition was reasonably related to the purpose of rehabilitation.[6]

One month after standing outside the postal office with the sandwich board, Gementera stole mail for the second time.[7] Gementera was again in front of Judge Walker, who expressed frustration that his original sentence had not "put [Gementera] on the right track."[8] This result raises an important question: what type of punishment would have put Gementera on the right track? As the Ninth Circuit noted in its decision affirming Judge Walker's signboard requirement, "much uncertainty exists as to how rehabilitation is best accomplished," and recidivism rates are unfortunately extremely high, regardless of the type of punishment.[9]

Some commentators argue that although public shaming sanctions were once effective, they are no longer useful because modern societal conditions do not foster an environment in which such punishments thrive.[10] Others argue that shaming sanctions are inherently cruel and socially unacceptable.[11] Nonetheless, courts continue to implement public shaming sanctions and the legal community has been unable to agree upon a common objection to them.[12]

As public shaming sanctions continue to be issued, one begins to wonder where they will go next. Over time, these sanctions have evolved from the placement of offenders in stocks, which restrained the offender's hands and feet between wooden boards,[13] to the positioning of the previously described offender in front of a post office wearing a signboard.[14] Further, some courts have taken these punishments to print media, requiring offenders to have their names and mug shots publicized.[15] Although Gementera became a repeat offender, it is unclear what caused this result. Gementera may have stolen mail again because his punishment included an inherently ineffective shaming punishment. On the other hand, perhaps that particular type of shaming punishment simply did not work. The judiciary has already shown vast creativity in sentencing, and it may be time to continue innovating.[16]

Believing that public shaming punishments generally have the ability to positively affect their children's behavior, parents have utilized public shaming punishments in much the same way as courts have.[17] Some parents have even taken to their children's social media profiles to punish their children because they believe that using social media as a means to punish might be effective in today's culture.[18] If parents are using this method of punishment, it may be time for the courts to take note. Gementera was twenty-four years old at the time he committed his crime, and had been a past offender since the age of eighteen.[19] People in this age group frequently use social media websites, such as Facebook.[20] What if Judge Walker's sentence had required Gementera to post his mug shot on his Facebook page accompanied by the caption, "I stole mail. This is my punishment"? This Note proposes that this type of shaming sanction might be an effective addition to the menu of public shaming punishments the judiciary already offers.[21]

Section II of this Note lays the foundation of shaming punishments in America, giving an overview of their history and development. Section III discusses the Ninth Circuit's recent decision in *Gementera*, in which the court upheld a modern-day public shaming punishment, as well as other select cases that have upheld public shaming punishments that involve print media. Section IV outlines the current scholarly debate surrounding the use of public shaming punishments. Section V gives an overview of the presence of social media and Internet usage in today's society, discusses a new trend among parents in which parents have begun to utilize social media to punish their children, and evaluates public shaming punishments via social media websites from the vantage point of various criminal law theories. Finally, Section VI advocates for the inclusion of online social media public shaming punishments into the judiciary's already expansive list of sentencing options, but with some limitations and guidelines.

The History of Public Shaming Punishments

Public Shaming Punishments in Colonial America

The Scarlet Letter illustrates the classic public shaming punishment, where the protagonist Hester Prynne must wear a scarlet letter "A" on her chest to represent her adulterous behavior.[22] In early America, shaming punishments were among the most popular methods of criminal sanctioning.[23] Vivid images of public punishments involving the stocks come to mind whereby the offender's hands and feet were restrained between wooden boards.[24] Sentences often included the requirement that the offender display a sign or write a letter announcing his wrongful behavior.[25] Flogging and branding were also used, but were considered more severe forms of public shaming punishments because they involved an element of physical pain.[26] The use of pillories, which were similar to the stocks except that the offender's head was also constrained,[27] seemingly developed to punish those criminals whose offenses did not warrant a harsh physical component. Arguably then, the only conceivable characteristic of punishment in the use of the pillory was for the purpose of public display, and thus humiliation.[28] In colonial America, these types of punishments were extremely common and the public usually participated in their administration.[29]

Scholars offer various theories as to why shaming sanctions were so popular during this time period. One theory rests on the fact that most American societies were small, close-knit communities in which people knew each other very well.[30] Any sort of public display emanating from a criminal's offense was utterly humiliating to offenders who knew the majority of the watchful crowd.[31] Consequently, community members would be aware of the offender's crime, spread this information to others, and criminals would thus feel the sting of shame.[32] Fear of public exposure and community disapproval made public shaming punishments extremely effective because it deterred crime and controlled deviant behavior.[33] However, these punishments were only successful because of "the community's familiarity with the offender and his recognized membership to the community";[34] if a wrongdoer did not have a connection with the community, public shaming sanctions would most likely not affect that criminal's behavior.[35]

A related explanation for the success of shaming punishments in early America stems from the limited mobility during this time period.[36] Most residents of small communities were life-long members who rarely contemplated moving elsewhere.[37] Thus, small communities that rarely diversified their membership perpetuated the ability for shaming punishments to have a powerful effect. Additionally, because imprisonment was expensive in the colonial period just as it is today, public shaming sanctions presented a cheaper form of punishment.[38] Therefore, public shaming punishments were preferable because they were inexpensive to administer and effective within immobile communities.

Finally, the presence of religion in colonial America played a large role in the effectiveness of shaming sanctions.[39] Community members were often "stern moralists" because of their strict religious beliefs.[40] Religious virtues infiltrated society and created "a clear manner in which citizens were expected to behave."[41] "Law and religion were so deeply intertwined that colonists even shaped their laws around their religious precepts, equating crime with sin."[42] If one was publicly shamed, it meant that he not only broke the written law but also the law of a higher power. Thus, a society in which the entire community held strong negative beliefs about criminal behavior created an environment in which shaming sanctions were extremely effective.

The combination of close-knit communities, lack of mobility among such communities, the cost-effectiveness of public shaming punishment, and the prevailing religious discipline of the time fostered an environment in which shaming punishments flourished. However, by the nineteenth century, public shaming sanctions had fallen out of favor.

[…]

The Future of the Use of Social Media Websites in Public Shaming Punishments

Public shaming sanctions that utilize social media websites are likely supported by criminal law theories. Further, such punishments have already been used by parents and seem to be effective in some instances. The question remains whether or not the judiciary should take the next step in expanding its already creative public shaming punishments to include punishments that utilize social media websites.

Noting the apparent inconsistency in sentencing that shaming punishments lead to, Professor Jonathan Turley has asserted that "judges are not chosen to serve as parents trying to set consequences for wayward children. Law demands not just consequences for wrongdoing, but consistent consequences. Otherwise citizens are left wondering whether they will receive a standard punishment or one improvised to suit a judge's whim."[252] The use of such customized punishments could undermine the criminal justice system's desire to make criminal sentencing more uniform.[253] Professor Turley asserts the legislature should be responsible for defining the ranges of permissible punishment.[254]

If the judiciary wishes to utilize online social media public shaming punishments, the public may indeed be better served if they are accompanied by legislative guidelines. The following parts do not provide a detailed statutory guideline, but rather a simplistic overview of some of the more important considerations legislatures should take into account.[255] Statutory guidelines should seek to address two main criticisms of these types of public shaming punishments: (A) that judicial discretion in this area will create inconsistent sentencing, and (B) that these types of punishments merely humiliate offenders and serve no rehabilitative purpose.

Statutory Guidelines to Avoid Sentencing Inconsistency

Even though the threat of sentencing inconsistency is present whenever judges have sentencing discretion, statutory guidelines could decrease the possibility of large discrepancies in sentencing when judges wish to utilize online social media public shaming punishments. As previously discussed, many people in the United States use social media; however, not all criminals will be able to be punished with an online social media public shaming punishment because they may not even have access to the Internet, let alone have an online social media presence.

Therefore, a sentencing guideline that requires judges to thoroughly investigate whether this type of public shaming punishment would be effective upon a particular offender should be encouraged.

In 1984, Congress passed the Sentencing Reform Act, which established the federal sentencing commission.[256] The U.S. Sentencing Commission was responsible for writing mandatory guidelines that judges had to follow when sentencing convicted criminals who had committed the same crimes.[257] However, in 2005, the Supreme Court ruled that United States Sentencing Guidelines were unconstitutional in the landmark case *United States v. Booker*.[258] Following *Booker*, the Guidelines became advisory, rather than mandatory.[259] This holding caused many people to worry that defendants would be treated unfairly as judges gained greater discretion in sentencing.[260] However, the Booker Court limited judicial discretion by requiring judges to "consult those Guidelines and take them into account when sentencing."[261]

Even though the Guidelines are no longer mandatory, many judges continue to sentence defendants within the sentencing ranges provided by the Guidelines.[262] In 2012, the United States Sentencing Commission released a report stating that the Guidelines "have remained the essential starting point for all federal sentences and have continued to influence sentences significantly."[263] Between December 2007 and October 2011, 80.7% of sentences fell within the Guideline ranges or fell below those ranges pursuant to a government motion.[264] Thus, even though the Guidelines are no longer mandatory, they continue to be extremely influential in a judge's decision-making process. As such, they stand to be a useful tool in formulating more consistent public shaming punishments.

In formulating online public shaming punishments, judges should not be able to impose punishments that require offenders to go out of their way to acquire computers or certain programs over the Internet in order to carry out their sentences. Judges should only implement public shaming conditions utilizing social media websites if the Government can prove that the offender already has access to the Internet and has an online social media presence. As discussed above, such a punishment will likely only be successful if the offender has created his own online community. Thus, judges should be required to evaluate the criminal and determine whether this type of punishment is appropriate for him or her. A guideline that codifies this requirement would help alleviate inconsistencies in sentencing because offenders would know in advance what type of punishment they could potentially receive. For example, an offender who is poor and does not have access to a computer would not be worried that this type of punishment could be enforced upon him. On the other hand, a more high profile or wealthy offender who has a large online social media presence would understand that committing a crime puts him at risk for such a punishment.

Further, the legislature should consider implementing a table of penalties outlining the offenses that could lead to the implementation of an online social media public shaming punishment. This implementation would again put potential offenders on notice of potential punishments. The table could also include the various types of online social media public shaming punishments that are available for the judiciary to use. This Note has only mentioned the use of an offender's Facebook through the posting of the offender's mug shot with a caption; however the legislature would be free to add other forms of punishments using other social media websites. For example, the judiciary could require an offender to "tweet" an apology to his followers on Twitter. However, if the Facebook punishment were the only one available, this would greatly limit sentencing inconsistencies between eligible offenders because only one punishment could be utilized amongst them. Thus, a sentencing guideline incorporating a table of penalties with types of online punishments and outlining necessary offender characteristics would serve to reduce sentencing inconsistencies in the context of online social media public shaming punishments.

Statutory Guidelines to Avoid Punishments
Solely for the Sake of Humiliation

In implementing public shaming sanctions via social media websites, sentencing guidelines that require such punishments to include reintegrative elements would eliminate the impression that the punishment was solely being used to humiliate the offender. Studies suggest that the effectiveness of shaming sanctions depends somewhat on whether a culture shames reintegratively, meaning that the community seeks to redeem the offender after the shaming has occurred and to reaccept that person into society.[265] The main difference between shaming that is reintegrative and shaming that is disintegrative is that disintegrative shaming seeks to stigmatize the offender in order to create a class of outcasts, while reintegrative shaming pays more attention to de-labeling the offender as a gesture of reacceptance and forgiveness.[266] One example where such reintegrative shaming occurs is within a family where the child does not become a criminal but rather knows that even after his punishment, his family will continue to love him.[267] It is hypothesized that "families are the most effective agents of social control" because of their use of this "continuum of love."[268] Thus, public shaming punishments that contain more reintegrative elements could have the effect of greater social control over criminals.

Although one commentator suggests that today's individualistic modern culture does not foster an environment of reintegration because communities do not have rituals to reclaim the offender,[269] it is not impossible to at least try to create such an environment. As another commentator more optimistically discusses, there is a possibility of devising shaming ceremonies that are reintegrative, rather than disintegrative.[270] For example, the rehabilitative subculture of Alcoholics Anonymous serves such a purpose in society "where those who perform remarkable feats of rehabilitation are held up as role models" and "where ceremonies to decertify deviance are widely understood and readily accessible."[271]

It certainly appears to be possible to formulate public shaming sanctions that foster a more reintegrative approach rather than a disintegrative one. As already seen in *Gementera*, Judge Walker created a probation condition that included a public shaming element as well as requirements for the offender to give lectures at schools and write letters to his victims.[272] This sort of combination of public shaming with reintegrative social elements appears to walk the line between a sanction that clearly seeks to condemn and ostracize the offender, with one that desires to redeem the offender and reclaim him back into society. Further, a reintegrative approach is possible when utilizing social media websites to publicly shame an offender. As demonstrated by Denise Abbott when she used her daughter's Facebook to shame her daughter, she also required her daughter to answer inquiries about what she had done wrong and to explain herself to anyone who asked.[273] This requirement forced her daughter to reflect on her actions, one of the first steps in rehabilitating an offender. Additionally, by requiring her daughter to make contact with those who knew her and were inquiring about her wrongdoing, her daughter was, in a way, being reaccepted amongst her peers. While it may be unrealistic to believe that the probation system could emulate this exact form of punishment as a probation condition, it can be argued that the mere act of requiring the offender to post his picture and an explanation of his crime online would itself be rehabilitative and open the door for his reintegration into society.

With the wide discretion that judges currently have in formulating punishments, there seems to be a place in the judicial system for reintegrative public shaming punishments that utilize social media websites. However, if the judiciary wishes to incorporate online social media public shaming sanctions into its existing punishment options, state legislatures and/or Congress should implement guidelines for such use.

Resources

1. *See, e.g.,* People v. McDowell, 130 Cal. Rptr. 839, 842–43 (Cal. Ct. App. 1976) (observing that a probation condition requiring a thief to wear tap shoes anytime he leaves the house is not constitutionally unreasonable merely because the condition is out of the ordinary); Goldschmitt v. State, 490 So. 2d 123, 124–25 (Fla. Dist. Ct. App. 1986) (concluding display of a bumper sticker that read "CONVICTED D.U.I.—RESTRICTED LICENSE" as part of defendant's punishment "is not necessarily offensive to the Constitution"); Ballenger v. State, 436 S.E.2d 793, 795 (Ga. Ct. App. 1993) (upholding a probation condition requiring the defendant to wear a fluorescent pink bracelet reading "D.U.I. CONVICT"); Ron Word, *Better Than Jail Time? Some Judges Try Unusual Sentences*, L.A. TIMES (Nov. 4, 2007), http://articles.latimes.com/2007/nov/04/news/adna-sentences4 (describing judicial sentences that include requiring offenders to wear signs articulating their crimes).

2. *See* United States v. Clark, 918 F.2d 843, 845, 848 (9th Cir. 1990) (concluding that a condition of probation for the defendant, a police officer convicted of perjury, to publish an apology in a local newspaper was not an abuse of discretion); Lindsay v. State, 606 So. 2d 652, 653–54, 658 (Fla. Dist. Ct. App. 1992) (upholding probation condition requiring probationer to place an advertisement in a local newspaper that consisted of the probationer's mug shot, name, and the caption "DUI—Convicted"); *see also* Jan Hoffman, *Crime and Punishment: Shame Gains Popularity*, N.Y. TIMES (Jan. 16, 1997), http://www.nytimes.com/1997/01/16/us/crimeand- punishment-shame-gains-popularity.html ("Convicted shoplifters must take out advertisements in their local newspapers, running their photographs and announcing their crimes.").

3. 379 F.3d 596 (9th Cir. 2004).

4. *Id*. at 598.

5. *Id*. at 605.

6. *Id*. at 607.

7. Pam Smith, *Scarlet Letter Sentence Doesn't Work*, 130 RECORDER 12, 12 (2006).

8. *Id*.

9. *Gementera*, 379 F.3d at 604. The court observed that "two-thirds of the 640,000 state and federal inmates who will be released in 2004 will return to prison within a few years." *Id*. (citing *The Price of Prisons*, N.Y. TIMES (June 26, 2004), http://www.nytimes .com/2004/06/26/opinion/the-price-of-prisons.html; BUREAU OF JUSTICE STATISTICS, DEP'T OF JUSTICE, NCJ 193427, RECIDIVISM OF PRISONERS RELEASED IN 1994, at 1 (2002) (finding a 67.5% recidivism rate within three years of release among study population of 300,000 prisoners released in 1994)).

10. Toni M. Massaro, *Shame, Culture, and American Criminal Law*, 89 MICH. L. REV. 1880, 1922–24 (1991).

11. *See* Jon A. Brilliant, Note, *The Modern Day Scarlet Letter: A Critical Analysis of Modern Probation Conditions*, 1989 DUKE L.J. 1357, 1382–84 (1989); *see also* Massaro, *supra* note 10, at 1942; James Q. Whitman, *What is Wrong With Inflicting Shame Sanctions?*, 107 YALE L.J. 1055, 1057 (1998).

12. *See* Whitman, *supra* note 11, at 1057. 13. ADAM JAY HIRSCH, THE RISE OF THE PENITENTIARY: PRISONS AND PUNISHMENT IN EARLY AMERICA 5 (1992).

14. *See* United States v. Gementera, 379 F.3d 596, 598 (9th Cir. 2004).

15. *See supra* note 2.

16. Innovation may come from within the court system, or even from local law enforcement. *See Gementera*, 379 F.3d at 610 (noting that "in comparison with the reality of the modern prison, we simply have no reason to conclude that the sanction . . . exceeds the bounds of 'civilized standards' or other 'evolving standards of decency that mark the progress of a maturing society'"); Philip Caulfield, *Huntington Beach, Calif., Plagued by*

Drunk Drivers, Considers Posting DUI Mugshots on Facebook, DAILY NEWS (Jan. 18, 2011, 9:22 AM), http://www. nydailynews.com/news/national/huntington-beach-calif -plagued-drunk-drivers-considers-posting-dui-mug shots-facebook-article-1.152163 (describing police department's consideration of shaming arrested, not convicted, drunk drivers by posting their mug shots on Facebook); Wes Venteicher, *Suburban Police Department to Tweet Names of DUI Suspects,* CHI. TRIB. (Dec. 10, 2013), http://articles .chicagotribune.com/2013-12-10/news/ chi-drunk-driving-tweets-riverside-20131210_1_ impaired-drivers-names-drunk-driving-arrests (discussing choice of police department to start tweeting information of anyone arrested of drunk driving).

17. *See infra* Section V.B.

18. *See infra* Section V.B.

19. *Gementera,* 379 F.3d at 598.

20. *See* David Cohen, *AllFacebook Stats Adds Data by Country,* ALLFACEBOOK (May 14, 2012, 11:50 AM), http://allfacebook.com/allfacebook-stats-by-country_b88679 (noting in a table that there are approximately eighteen million male Facebook users between the ages of eighteen and twenty-four).

21. This Note's discussion and analysis assume that the particular offender actually has an online social media presence. An argument can be made that public shaming sanctions involving the use of social media will be ineffective because such punishments will have no use in relation to certain criminals, particularly those who are poor and have no Internet access. However, at most, this consideration just advances the argument that the judiciary should be *selective* in imposing such sanctions. *See infra* Section VI. Further, it seems unlikely that all potential offenders in a class of criminals, including drunk drivers, embezzlers, thieves, or rapists, would escape the reach of this sort of shaming sanction. As a particular illustration of the pervasiveness of social media as of 2014, approximately 1.35 billion people use Facebook each month. *Newsroom,* FACEBOOK, http://newsroom.fb .com/Key-Facts (last updated Sep. 30, 2014). Additionally, as of 2012, approximately 173 million people subscribed to Facebook in North America. *Facebook Users in the World: Facebook Usage and Facebook Growth Statistics by World Geographic Regions,* INTERNET WORLD STATS, http://www.internetworldstats.com/facebook. htm (last visited Dec. 22, 2014). These numbers have been on the rise each year, even in developing nations. *Id.*

22. NATHANIEL HAWTHORNE, THE SCARLET LETTER (Bill Blauvelt, ed., Townsend Press, 2007) (1850).

23. LAWRENCE M. FRIEDMAN, CRIME AND PUNISHMENT IN AMERICAN HISTORY 38 (1993) (noting that shaming punishments were used with great frequency in colonial America).

24. HIRSCH, *supra* note 13, at 5; Whitman, supra note 11, at 1060–61 (1998) (noting that flogging and using the pillory and stocks were regarded as shaming sanctions in the seventeenth and eighteenth centuries).

25. *See* Massaro, *supra* note 10, at 1913–14 (outlining common techniques to publicly shame offender).

26. FRIEDMAN, *supra* note 23, at 40 (observing that branding was used to mark an offender to the public); HIRSCH, *supra* note 13, at 5 (noting the use of branding to warn the community of a person's criminal propensities); Brilliant, *supra* note 11, at 1361 (describing the use of branding and flogging in American colonies); Massaro, *supra* note 10, at 1913 (discussing how branding and maiming effectively cast the offender out of the community).

27. HIRSCH, *supra* note 13, at 5.

28. HARRY ELMER BARNES, THE STORY OF PUNISHMENT: A RECORD OF MAN'S INHUMANITY TO MAN 62–63 (2d ed. 1972) ("When the pillory was employed in a

simple fashion and not accompanied by any other mode of punishment, its operation was chiefly psychological, and it was designed to bring about the feeling of humiliation naturally attendant upon the infliction of public disgrace."); *see* Scott E. Sanders, *Scarlet Letters, Bilboes and Cable TV: Are Shame Punishments Cruel and Outdated or Are They a Viable Option for American Jurisprudence?*, 37 WASHBURN L.J. 359, 363 (1998) ("While the physical abuse was severe, the accompanying shame was often the most painful ingredient of the punishment.").

29. Dan M. Kahan, *What Do Alternative Sanctions Mean*, 63 U. CHI. L. REV. 591, 611 (1996); *see* HIRSCH, *supra* note 13, at 5 (noting that public shaming was performed before the assembled community on market or lecture days).

30. *See* MICHAEL STEPHEN HINDUS, PRISON AND PLANTATION: CRIME, JUSTICE, AND AUTHORITY IN MASSACHUSETTS AND SOUTH CAROLINA 1767-1878, at 100–01 (1980); Aaron S. Book, Note, *Shame on You: An Analysis of Modern Shame Punishment as an Alternative to Incarceration*, 40 WM. & MARY L. REV. 653, 658 (1999) (noting that the first shame sanctions responded to the closeness of communities); *see also* Massaro, *supra* note 10, at 1916 (explaining that the offender needs to be part of a group for shaming to be effective).

31. HIRSCH, *supra* note 13, at 34 ("The sting of the lash and the contortions of the stocks were surely no balm, but even worse for community members were the piercing stares of neighbors who witnessed their disgrace and with whom they would continue to live and work."); *see also* Massaro, *supra* note 10, at 1902, 1916.

32. Deni Smith Garcia, *Three Worlds Collide: A Novel Approach to the Law, Literature, and Psychology of Shame*, 6 TEX. WESLEYAN L. REV. 105, 111 (1999) (noting that an offender must be a member of a group whose members know of the shaming and that the group must actually shun the offender); Massaro, *supra* note 10, at 1902 (describing the necessity of offender communicating shame to the group, the group's actual knowledge of the act, and group withdrawal and how important community perception and disapproval were to offenders); *see* HIRSCH, *supra* note 13, at 34 (observing that offenders felt shame when they knew and respected their onlookers).

33. *See* Phaedra Athena O'Hara Kelly, Comment, *The Ideology of Shame: An Analysis of First Amendment and Eighth Amendment Challenges to Scarlet-Letter Probation Conditions*, 77 N.C. L. REV. 783, 805 (1998) (noting the large fear of "losing face" among community members); *see also* Sanders, *supra* note 28, at 361 ("In colonial America, shame punishments led to shunning by the community, a high price to pay in New England's close-knit communities."); Leslie Cannold, *Power of Shame Rules Our Actions*, THE AGE (Jan. 11, 2014), http://www.theage. com.au/comment/power-of-shame-rules -our-actions-20140110-30mc7.html (explaining that shaming is an effective form of social control because individuals care about what others think).

34. Barbara Clare Morton, Note, *Bringing Skeletons Out of the Closet and into the Light— "Scarlet Letter" Sentencing Can Meet the Goals of Probation in Modern America Because It Deprives Offenders of Privacy*, 35 SUFFOLK U. L. REV. 97, 103 (2001); *see* HIRSCH, *supra* note 13, at 34 (arguing that the communal character of colonial American towns fostered an environment in which public shaming was effective).

35. HINDUS, *supra* note 30, at 100–01 (describing the reasons why public shaming punishments fell out of use in Massachusetts in the early nineteenth century but continued in South Carolina, "a relatively stable rural state where face-to-face contact remained important and where honor was accorded great protection"); HIRSCH, *supra* note 13, at 40 (arguing that public shaming failed when the offender lacked community ties); Massaro, *supra* note 10, at 1903 (noting that shaming loses its sting if the audience ignores the public spectacle).

36. Morton, *supra* note 34, at 103; *see* HIRSCH, *supra* note 13, at 32 (noting the limited mobility in early colonial America).

37. Morton, *supra* note 34, at 103; *see* HIRSCH, *supra* note 13, at 32–33 (noting the existence of life-long residents in many towns that experienced little turnover in population).

38. *See* HIRSCH, *supra* note 13, at 8.

39. Morton, *supra* note 34, at 103; *see* Sanders, *supra* note 28, at 361–62 (asserting that religion played a "heavy role in the colonial philosophy of punishment").

40. Morton, *supra* note 34, at 103.

41. *Id.* at 104.

42. *Id.* at 103.

252. Turley, *supra* note 70.

253. *Id.*

254. *Id.*

255. For another perspective outlining how the judicial system should implement public shaming sanctions, *see* Book, *supra* note 30, at 681–86.

256. Mosi Secret, *Wide Sentencing Disparity Found Among U.S. Judges,* N.Y. TIMES (Mar. 5, 2012), http://www.nytimes.com/2012/03/06/nyregion/wide-sentencing-disparity -found-among-us-judges.html.

257. *Id.*

258. 543 U.S. 220, 245 (2005).

259. *See id.*

260. Secret, *supra* note 256.

261. *Booker,* 543 U.S. at 264.

262. Ken LaMance, *How Federal Sentencing Guidelines Have Recently Changed,* LEGALMATCH, http://www. legalmatch.com/law-library/article/how-federal-sentencing -guidelines-have-recently-changed.html (last modified Jan. 27, 2012); Secret, supra note 256.

263. UNITED STATES SENTENCING COMMISSION, REPORT ON THE CONTINUING IMPACT OF *UNITED STATES V. BOOKER* ON FEDERAL SENTENCING 60 (2012), *available at* http://www.ussc.gov/sites/default/files/pdf/news/ congressionaltestimony- and-reports/booker-reports/2012-booker/Part_A.pdf.

264. *Id.* at 5, 60.

265. JOHN BRAITHWAITE, CRIME, SHAME AND REINTEGRATION 55 (1989); Massaro, *supra* note 10, at 1924.

266. BRAITHWAITE, *supra* note 265, at 55.

267. *Id.* at 56 (discussing the "family model").

268. *Id.*

269. Massaro, *supra* note 10, at 1924 ("The earmarks of reintegrative shame cultures include social cohesiveness, a strong family system, high communitarianism, and social control mechanisms that aim to control by reintegration into the cohesive networks, rather than by formal restraint.").

270. BRAITHWAITE, *supra* note 265, at 163.

271. *Id.*

272. United States v. Gementera, 379 F.3d 596, 599 (9th Cir. 2004).

273. *See* Doty, *supra* note 207.

> *"Shame might cause some people to blame others, but it could lead others toward rehabilitation and a brighter future."*

Shaming Can Reduce Recidivism

Wray Herbert

In the following viewpoint, Wray Herbert cites early research suggesting that public shaming may in fact lead criminals to less repeat offenses. Herbert is optimistic that shame may be an effective tool to change behavior, but only for those who take accountability for their actions. However, due to a small sample size and inconclusive results, Herbert cautions against placing too much faith in shaming practices. In addition, some who avoid repeating crimes may simply be in temporary hiding. More study is required to determine how shaming effects recidivism. Wray Herbert has been writing about psychology and human behavior for more than twenty-five years. He has been the behavioral science editor at Science News *and the editor-in-chief of* Psychology Today.

As you read, consider the following questions:

1. How does the author distinguish between shame and guilt?
2. Why is guilt often thought to be a more productive emotion for rehabilitation purposes?
3. What evidence suggests that shame may not lead to long-term rehabilitation?

Twenty-four year old Shawn Gementera was caught red-handed pilfering letters from private mailboxes along San Francisco's Fulton Street. Mail theft is a serious crime, and it was not Gementera's first run-in with the law. Even so, the judge opted for a lenient sentence—just two months in jail and three years of supervised release. But the supervised release came with an unusual condition.

Gementera's sentence required him to stand in front of a San Francisco post office, wearing a sandwich board with these words in large letters: "I stole mail. This is my punishment." The convicted thief fought this provision, arguing that such public humiliation was cruel and unusual punishment, but he lost his appeal. The court argued that public humiliation was the point—not humiliation for the sake of humiliation, but as a deterrent against future crime.

This case took place a few years ago, but the idea of public shaming has a long history, dating back at least to the stockades of colonial times. This moral and legal sanction was immortalized in the fictional case of Hester Prynne, the main character of Nathaniel Hawthorne's *The Scarlet Letter*, who was condemned to wear the prominent 'A' for her crime of adultery. Such shaming punishments—sometimes called Scarlet Letter sentences—are making something of a comeback in recent years, raising not only legal but psychological questions as well, most notably: Do they work? Does forced public humiliation contribute to rehabilitation of criminal minds—and diminish the chances of repeat offenses?

The answers to these questions are unknown, and indeed the questions have not been well studied—at least not in the most relevant population, convicted criminals. Until now, that is. George Mason University clinical psychologist June Tangney recently conducted a study of shame in jail inmates, following them from soon after incarceration to about a year after their release. She wanted to see if in-mates who experienced shame were more or less likely to commit more crimes later on. More specifically, she wanted to compare the effects of shame and another self-conscious emotion, guilt, in rehabilitating criminals.

The distinction between shame and guilt may seem at first like semantic hair-splitting, but it's actually very important in studying punishment and rehabilitation. Feelings of guilt are focused on a particular act: "I did a bad thing by stealing other people's mail." By contrast, feelings of shame focus painfully on the self: "I am a bad person because I stole others' letters." When people are guilty—as proclaimed by a judge, for example—they experience remorse and regret, and they want to make reparations. But people who are shamed feel generally diminished, worthless—and defensive. Humiliated people want to slink into hiding, deny responsibility and, most important, blame others for what they did.

For this reason, Tangney expected that shame would be less effective than guilt in deterring future crime. That's because a bad, defective person is much worse—and harder to fix—than a bad behavior. She recruited more than 400 inmates at a local jail, all recently incarcerated on felony charges. She administered a standard assessment to identify which inmates were prone to guilt feelings and which to feelings of shame. It also identified those who most likely to blame others for their problems.

The in-mates then served their time and were released. About a year after release, Tangney and her colleagues followed up, to see how they were doing. They used several different measures, including self-reports and public records, to come up with a recidivism score for each inmate. She predicted that the shame-prone inmates—because of their tendency to assign blame rather than accept responsibility—would be more likely to return to crime after their release.

And that's what they found—at least when they first looked at the data. Shame did indeed cause former inmates to blame others for their misfortune, which in turn kept them from learning from their mistakes—and led to repeat crimes. By contrast, those who felt guilty at incarceration were much less likely to have relapsed a year later.

But further analysis revealed a much more nuanced view of shame. As reported in an article to appear in the journal *Psychological Science*, shame led to recidivism *only* when the humiliated inmates blamed others. When they did not—when they were humiliated yet accepted blame—inmates were no more likely to return to crime. In other words, the experience of shame is in some ways a liability, but in other ways it is adaptive, perhaps even a strength.

Here's the most intriguing finding. Apparently it's the powerful desire to hide away that determines shame's effects. People who are experiencing shame want to avoid others, and it may be that shame-prone ex-offenders do just that—withdraw from everyone, including their partners in crime, and thus stay clean. Or they might use their jail time to hunker down and think; they anticipate future shame, which has a deterrent effect on criminal activity. So shame might cause some people to blame others, but it could lead others toward rehabilitation and a brighter future. Shame, it seems, has two faces, both of which must be considered in attempts at restorative justice.

> *"The prospect of facing public humiliation could perhaps serve as a stronger deterrent than more 'severe' punishments like imprisonment or probation."*

Humiliation Is Appropriate in Certain Circumstances

John Richards

In the following viewpoint, John Richards provides a limited and conditional endorsement of pubic shaming. Such punishment is constitutional, since "cruel and unusual" punishment can evolve according to societal standards. Richards believes that shaming "in lieu of jail time, is an appropriate punishment for some crimes, under certain circumstances." Of course, this leaves open to discussion what these circumstances might look like. For instance, the author believes that minor offenses such as shirking jury duty should be punishable by shaming. He does, however, caution against shaming punishments turning inadvertently cruel. John Richards writes about legal affairs for Legal Match.

"Should Public Shaming Be an Option for Criminal Punishment?" John Richards, Legalmatch.com, February 3, 2012. Reprinted by permission.

As you read, consider the following questions:

1. Where does the author stand on whether or not public shaming constitutes cruel and unusual punishment?

2. Why doesn't the constitution more specifically define terms such as "cruel and unusual" or "unreasonable search and seizure"?

3. What are some dangers with public shaming penalties?

Implicit in most forms of criminal punishment is an element of public shame. Trials are generally visible to the public, and the convictions and sentences become a matter of public record, for the entire world to see. On the public record for years to come is a clear statement by a court saying something to the effect of "this person broke our society's rules, and is being punished for it."

However, we've generally shied away from more direct and literal forms of public shame for punishment. Adulterers no longer have to wear a scarlet letter. Petty thieves are no longer put in the stocks. However, in recent years, it seems that literal public shaming is coming back into vogue.

In the case linked above, a judge ordered a man who skipped out on jury duty to stand outside the courthouse for two days, holding a sign that read "I failed to appear for jury duty." This is similar to what other judges have done. Occasionally, judges will order shoplifters and other petty criminals (especially young people who are first offenders) to stand in front of the business they stole from holding a sign telling the world what they've done.

But, are such punishments appropriate? And, with respect to the issue in this particular case, should we re-think the whole concept of mandatory jury duty?

First, the question of public humiliation as punishment: is it constitutional? And is it effective?

The principle behind public humiliation as punishment is simple enough: people don't like being humiliated, and the prospect of facing public humiliation could perhaps serve as a stronger deterrent than more "severe" punishments like imprisonment or probation. And, enforcing a court order to stand outside a business holding a sign for a few weeks is probably far cheaper for the state than keeping a person in prison or on probation for months or years.

But even if you grant that public humiliation is effective, there's the question of whether or not it's constitutional. The 8th Amendment to the Constitution prohibits the government from imposing "cruel and unusual punishment." However, as with many other important terms in the Constitution (such as "due process of law," "unreasonable search and seizure," and "free exercise of religion"), the text of the Constitution doesn't bother to define the term. This was probably deliberate, as it gives courts leeway to adapt constitutional principles to evolving societal standards.

Personally, I think being required to stand in a public place a few hours a day for a few days or weeks holding a sign announcing to the world what they've done, especially when it's in lieu of jail time, is an appropriate punishment for some crimes, under certain circumstances.

There should be some basic safeguards in place to ensure that these punishments do not become cruel and unusual. For instance, a police officer should be present the whole time to monitor the offender's compliance with the sentence. But, just as importantly, they would be there to protect the offender from violence committed by others. If punishments that center on public humiliation amount to a tacit endorsement of vigilante justice, it would quickly become unconstitutional. Likewise, allowances should be made for severe weather. If a person is forced to stand outside in freezing weather, developing hypothermia or frostbite, they'll have been subjected to a punishment that is extremely excessive for the crime.

The case linked above also raises some issues about mandatory jury service, though the juror in question isn't exactly the most sympathetic person: he's unemployed, and admitted that he skipped out on jury duty because he wasn't paying attention to the judge,

WE AND THEY

In a few small towns of the American Northwest, certain criminals are getting "scarlet letter" treatment. Selected felons and misdemeanor offenders are being given the choice of public humiliation as an alternative to jail terms. Public humiliation is achieved through advertisements in local newspapers presenting the details of the offense, past criminal record, and a signed apology.

Thomas J. Bernard, a professor of criminal justice at Pennsylvania State University, says he does not think public humiliation would be very effective in heavily populated areas.

Oklahoma's Judge [Gary] Lumpkin notes, "I would imagine the 'lost in the crowd' type mentality would dilute the effect, unless there was some other way you brought it to public's attention."

Professor Bernard argues that "all this is public record anyway ... but if you institute a policy of this sort, several matters of fairness must be taken into account."

He says that defendants must be given adequate notification of the alternatives, use of public humiliation must be consistently applied, and that it should take place only after conviction, not simply because someone has been arrested and charged.

Although little research has been done on the subject, Bernard says, "stigma-type punishments are pretty effective with people who consider themselves law-abiding citizens."

But some experts are not so sure about the potential effects of such a program. "All this model does is reinforce how bad `they' are," says Judith Schloegel, director of the National Center for Innovations in Corrections in Washington, D.C. "It sets up a dichotomy between 'we and they.'"

"Choosing Between Public Humiliation and Jail," Kerry Elizabeth Knobelsdorff, *The Christian Science Monitor,* **January 2, 1987.**

and didn't realize that he had to return after the court adjourned for lunch. Being unemployed, it's not as if he had anything else to do. And he probably could have used the money that jury service pays (even if it is a pittance of 10-20 dollars a day).

However, in many other cases, mandatory jury service can represent a significant hardship, which is often overlooked. And courts and commentators are often very cavalier about the burden that jury duty can place on ordinary people, often resorting to lectures about civic duty which can just come off as pious and out-of-touch, without offering suggestions on how to mitigate these issues.

Of course, I'm not advocating the abolition of jury service (that would be impossible without eliminating the right to trial by jury), but I think it could be in need of a few commonsense reforms. One of the biggest complaints about mandatory jury service is that it requires people to skip work, often giving up their pay. Only a small minority of states require employers to pay employees while they're on jury duty. And while most states do pay jurors, the amount is usually insultingly low, considering the importance of the role that jurors play, and the burden that jury service can present. At the very least, jurors should be paid minimum wage for their service. Usually, they are paid far less than that.

If a juror is employed, perhaps employers could be required to contribute a portion of this sum, so the taxpayers do not have to shoulder the entire financial burden. And by making jury service slightly less burdensome and inconvenient, we would probably decrease the number of people who try to get out of jury duty, making it less likely that juries are going to be composed of people who resent being there, and therefore don't take their responsibilities seriously.

Jurors are the backbone of our legal system, and any measures encouraging them to take their duties seriously should be given serious consideration.

Periodical and Internet Sources Bibliography

The following articles have been selected to supplement the diverse views presented in this chapter.

John Anderson, "Public Shaming Is an Effective Alternative to Prison," The Daily Aztec, January 23, 2011. http://www .thedailyaztec.com/2088/opinion/public-shaming-is-an-effective -alternative-to-prison.

Lawyers.com, "Shame on You: Do 'Shaming' Punishments Work?" Retrieved September 2016. http://criminal.lawyers.com/criminal -law-basics/shame-on-you-do-shaming-punishments-work.html.

Magdeline Lum, "Public Shaming for the Greater Good," *Australasian Science*, Retrieved September 2016. http://www .australasianscience.com.au/article/issue-september-2011/public -shaming-greater-good.html.

Brian Palmer, "Can We Bring Back the Stockades?" Slate, November 15, 2012. http://www.slate.com/articles/news_and_politics/ explainer/2012/11/public_shaming_sentences_can_judges_ subject_criminals_to_humiliation.html.

John Richards, "Should Public Shaming Be an Option for Criminal Punishment?" Legal Match, February 3, 2012. http://lawblog .legalmatch.com/2012/02/03/public-shaming-option-criminal -punishment.

For Further Discussion

Chapter 1

1. Do you think public shaming can force institutions and corporations to behave better? Why or why not?
2. How might the internet's tendency to polarize discourse be remedied? Is this likely to happen?
3. Do you think individuals who say inappropriate things deserve to be shamed? How do you see the public/private divide online?

Chapter 2

1. How do racial and class backgrounds influence the way parents integrate online shaming into their child rearing?
2. Is there a place for mild shaming in school or work? Have we become too thin-skinned? Or is shaming purely negative for psychological development?
3. Do you think observing a shaming episode is inherently cruel? Why or why not?

Chapter 3

1. What do you think motivates those who shame individuals on social media? Do you think they are seeking personal fame or trying to influence people at large to behave better? Or both? Is it justified?
2. Do you think the threat of being shamed is an effective corrective on behavior? Or do you agree with some commentators who claim that racists will only be emboldened by negative fallout?

3. Is it fair for journalists to use their platform to shame others? Should journalists and other media professionals be held to a higher standard?

Chapter 4

1. With so many problems associated with the so-called prison industrial complex, do you agree with judges who use public shaming as an alternative form of punishment? Why or why not?
2. Are there other approaches to judicial punishment that may be more effective than shame? If so, how can we encourage their use by judges?
3. How do we determine what is cruel and unusual punishment, and how does technology affect how these standards evolve? Do you think public shaming is constitutional in a judicial context?

Organizations to Contact

The editors have compiled the following list of organizations concerned with the issues debated in this book. The descriptions are derived from materials provided by the organizations. All have publications or information available for interested readers. The list was compiled on the date of publication of the present volume; the information provided here may change. Be aware that many organizations take several weeks or longer to respond to inquiries, so allow as much time as possible.

End to Cyber Bullying
147 West 35th Street, Suite 1404
New York, NY 10001
(772) 202-ETCB (3822)
email: info@endcyberbullying.com
website: http://www.endcyberbullying.org

Founded on May 1, 2011, End to Cyber Bullying (ETCB) is a nonprofit organization aimed at combating cyberbullying in this modern age of advancing technology. Its mission is to raise awareness, provide information on cyberbullying, offer compassionate, approachable services, and mobilize students, educators, parents, and others in taking efforts to end cyberbullying.

Hello, Racist!
email: http://helloracist.com/contact
website: http://helloracist.com

Hello, Racist! is an organization devoted to exposing racist behavior and fighting ignorance. As its method is to expose and shame individuals committing these acts, please be aware that this is a "pro-shaming" site.

PACER's National Bullying Prevention Center
8161 Normandale Blvd.
Bloomington, MN 55437
(800) 537-2237
website: www.pacer.org

PACER's National Bullying Prevention Center actively leads social change, so that bullying is no longer considered an accepted childhood rite of passage. PACER provides innovative resources for students, parents, educators, and others, and recognizes bullying as a serious community issue that impacts education, physical and emotional health, and the safety and well-being of students.

Parenting Beyond Punishment
PO Box 29223
Atlanta, GA 30359
email: amy@parentingbeyondpunishment.com
website: http://parentingbeyondpunishment.com/contact

Parenting Beyond Punishment is an organization and resource devoted to peaceful parenting. This is the use of intentional, gentle ways to guide children using empathetic and cooperative solutions versus trying to control their behavior with bribes, yelling, and punishments. It involves working with children by listening, understanding, responding, and communicating with intention.

Stomp Out Bullying
(877) NOBULLY (877 602 8559)
website: www.stompoutbullying.org

Stomp Out Bullying is the leading national anti-bullying and cyberbullying organization for kids and teens in the U.S. Stomp Out Bullying focuses on reducing and preventing bullying, cyberbullying, sexting and other digital abuse, educating against homophobia, racism and hatred, decreasing school absenteeism, and deterring violence in schools, online and in communities across the country.

Stopbullying.gov
U.S. Department of Health & Human Services
200 Independence Avenue, S.W.
Washington, D.C. 20201
website: www.stopbullying.gov

StopBullying.gov provides information from various government agencies on what bullying is, what cyberbullying is, who is at risk, and how you can prevent and respond to bullying. The StopBullying.gov coordinates closely with the Federal Partners in Bullying Prevention Steering Committee, an interagency effort led by the Department of Education that works to coordinate policy, research, and communications on bullying topics.

Bibliography of Books

David Brake, *Sharing Our Lives Online: Risks and Exposure in Social Media*. New York, NY: Palgrave Macmillan, 2014.

George Caspar, *Shame and Internet Trolling: A Personal Exploration of the Mindset Behind This Modern Behavior*. BookBaby, 2014.

Shari Mabry Gordon, *Are You at Risk for Public Shaming?* New York, NY: Enslow, 2016.

Rober E. Gutsche, *Media Control: News as an Institution of Power and Social Control*. New York, NY: Bloomsbury Academic, 2015.

Jack Lasky, *America's Prisons*. Farmington Hills, MI: Greenhaven Press, 2016.

Laura Martocci, *Bullying: The Social Destruction of Self*. Philadelphia, PA: Temple University Press, 2015.

Anne Marie McAlinden, *The Shaming of Sexual Offenders: Risk, Retribution, and Reintegration*. Portland, OR: Hart, 2007.

Peter Moskos, *In Defense of Flogging*. New York, NY: Basic Books, 2011.

Julian Petley, *Media and Public Shaming: Drawing the Boundaries of Disclosure*. New York, NY: Palgrave Macmillan, 2013.

Jon Ronson, *So You've Been Publicly Shamed*. New York, NY: Riverhead Books, 2015.

Nancy Jo Sales, *American Girls: Social Media and the Secret Lives of Teenagers*. New York, NY: Alfred A. Knopf, 2016.

Benedicte Sere and Jorg Wettlaufer, *Shame Between Punishment and Penance*. Firenze, Italy: SISMEL, 2013.

Index